Farewell, My Friend

A Step-by-Step Guide to Handling a Serious
Illness and Even the Death of a Loved One

Deacon Young

Best Wishes & God Bless

Beatrice Toney Bailey

8/15/09

Beatrice Toney Bailey

"Farewell, My Friend"

Written by: Beatrice Toney Bailey
                     Bedaparlé

Edited by:

                     Wendy Ellison-Allen
                     Charley Blatchford
                     Judy Blatchford
                     Gladys Washington
                     Deborah Nelson

Printed by: Sheridan Books, Inc
                     First Printing April 2008
                     Printed in the United States of America

Cover Design by Mustang Graphics.
Cover Photo, "Farewell, My Friend", by Carl W. Nunn, imagesbynunn.com
Back Cover Photo, Patrick Preyer.
Author's Hairstyle by Carla preyer, Inner Beauty Design.

IBSN: 978-0-9801520-0-5

First Printing: April 2008
Printed in the United States of America

"Farewell, My Friend" can be ordered as follows:
farewellmyfriend.net
Beatrice Toney Bailey
Bedaparlé
PO Box 2444
Citrus Heights, CA 95611-2444
1-916-745-3454

Dedication

May 1938 – June 2006

This book is dedicated to my husband, Richard James Bailey, Sr.,
who, sadly, made this book possible.

Table of Contents

Table of Contents
(Continued)

Table of Contents
(Continued)

Table of Contents

(Continued)

Special Acknowledgments

There is nothing that I have accomplished or will accomplish
that I could have done or will do without the unmerited
Grace and Mercy of Jesus Christ.

This book is also dedicated to my wonderful family:
My daughter, Wendy (Goosie) Allen, who encouraged, pushed, and supported me
throughout the inception and completion of this book;
my son, Rodney (Champy) Ellison II; who tenderly handled Rick's final details,
my daughter-in-law, Nao Qui (Nokie) Ellison; my son-in-law, Roy Allen;
and my grandchildren, Sascha, Rodney III (Punkin),
Isaac, Christopher, and Maxwell.

I would not have been able to handle this situation without the encouragement of my
sisters, Ellouise Clayvon, Diane Keating, Deborah Nelson, their spouses; and my
brother, Wendell Nance; sister-in-law, Linda Johnston; and brother-in-law Jim Douglas,
and my niece, Monique Nelson.
They were all very supportive to both Rick and me.

In addition to my family, my dear friends also talked me off the many emotional ledges
that I found myself on from time to time: Ruth (Rayuth) and Larry; Rosemary (R²);
Sharon (Q-Tip); Phyllis (Phyyllisss) and Don; Marchand and Clint;
Cindy and Michael, Dunice and Aubrey, Bruno and Chenita, Sandra, Mona
(MeeeeOhNaaaaa); Joan (Junior); Liz; Nancy and Dan; Diana (Lady Di);
and my St. Paul Baptist Church Family, including Pastor Ephraim Williams and
Sister Sue; SAG #11 Sisters; Coco and Phyllis; Sandra H.;
the Senior Usher Board Ministry; Carla (Inner Beauty);
RJ Bailey, Jr., my "bonus" son;
Jake, my friend and personal fitness trainer;
Charley, Judy, and Gladys who were both my friends and editors,
Kathy. who gave me the sub- title for this book, Dawwii N Fume, my friend,
and Carl, who took the book cover photo, "Farewell, My Friend."

A heart-felt thank you to all of you, who over the course of Rick's illness—from the date
of his back surgery until the day he died—either sent a card, e-mailed me a motivational
story; called to check on us, dropped off a dish of food,
and prayed individually and collectively for us.

A special thanks to the entire Kaiser Hospice staff that assisted us, particularly
Ardys, Ellen, and Alex. They are truly angels working amongst us.
Thank you Visiting Angels staff members Karen, Isabel, Altha
and, especially, LaCressia for the wonderful in-home care they gave to Rick.

I am who I am today due, in part, to many of the people who have crossed my path
whose first name started with an **"R".**
You all have proven to have been in my life for both my growth and pruning.

Foreword

Rick's battle with lung cancer was an arduous journey for both of us. It is a journey that many other people have or will have to take during their lifetime. This book is intended to be a guide to assist you in managing the many details associated with an illness and, sadly, the death of a loved one. Although I have tried to take different situations into consideration, this book does tend to lean towards the death of a spouse.

Throughout Rick's illness and until his ultimate death, many people said to me, *"I wouldn't know what to do, IF this happened to me."* It is not a matter of *"if"* you will have to deal with this subject, but *"when"*. This book is the result of hearing this type of comment over and over again. Your loved one dying first may not be part of your plan, but it may happen and you need to be prepared. I am confident that the information contained within this book will help you or your loved one find some order and peace of mind amidst your personal medical crisis. It will also allow you to avoid the many shocks and surprises that will be the result of not being properly prepared for the inevitable. Throughout this book you will find samples of the forms I have created to help me keep track of the many aspects of Rick's health care. There are blank copies of these forms at the end of each section that should be used to capture any action items on each section. If you want to have an electronic version of these forms, please go to my website and download the desired form. My website is wwwfarewellmyfriend.net.

If you are a part of the Baby Boomer generation, as I am, it is inevitable that you will be tackling a serious illness or burying a parent, a spouse, family member, or friend. But guess what, you don't have to be 45+ to have to go through what we have gone through. All or part of these challenges will show up at your doorstep one day. It is just a natural part of the circle of life and cannot be avoided. *__You owe it to yourself to read this book and pre-stage many of these suggested actions in order to get ahead of the curve for yourself and your loved ones__*. Planning to complete these actions "one of these days" translates to "none of these days."

I am not a doctor, a nurse, or an attorney, but have been a caregiver who has recently gone through the illness and death of a spouse. In trying to handle Rick's illness and keep my wits about me, I could not find a book that *handled all aspects* of a chronic illness and ultimately the burial of a loved one. As a result, I decided to write one. I don't have ALL of the answers, but I do want to share many that worked for me. It is my hope that some of this information will create "light bulb" moments in which you will find a way to make your life a bit easier. I have learned way too much during this process to keep it to myself. You will find some "off-the-wall" humor laced throughout the book because it is a part of who I am and was a good release of tension during this time.

The end result of following some or all of the advice offered will allow you to find some order in a personal sea of chaos.

Bea Bailey

You will never know what life will place on your doorstep...

OK, here I was. I had beaten the odds of a 40-something woman marrying for the second time around when "good" men were so hard to find. I once read a statistic that said that you have a better chance of being kidnapped by terrorists than marrying again at the age of 40. Well, I found one and I was the apple of his eye. Rick was from Connecticut and had been in the Armed Services for 30 years. He was a very intelligent man and an avid reader. Rick was proud of his Native American heritage and was half Iroquois, which is part of the Schagticoke Indian Nation. We were two distinctly different personalities. I was the type of person that would burst into a room and say, "Here I am!" and Rick was the type that would quietly enter a room and say, "Ah, there you are!" We married in 1993 and life was just a bowl of cherries. My son, Rodney, said that Rick and I looked so much alike that if we had a child together, it would look like Big Bird from *Sesame Street*!

We were both retired and had so many plans—to travel, travel, and then do some more traveling. We would go for walks around our home. I am an admitted Type "A" personality and you will see this sometimes manic behavior throughout this book. You will need either a Valium or 180 Proof Scotch to spend time with me on some days. When Rick and I would go for walks, I would start out with him and outpace him regularly. Not at first, because he could out walk me once he got going. Rick was not an overweight person and could do anything, once he put his mind to it. I knew that walking in our neighborhood wasn't the first thing that he wanted to be doing. The History Channel and/or the Military Channel were his friends and he liked to spend a lot of time with these friends.

Once I retired, we would go to the movies by ourselves or with Ruth and Larry, who were also retired. You ever notice how many grey-haired people are at the matinees? We also would play cards during the day with fellow retirees Bruno and Chenita when other poor souls would be slaving at work. Lots of bragging rights were given during competitive games of Shanghai, Leroy and 99-Back! We had good times sitting around a card table, eating homemade pie and wondering what the working stiffs were doing at 10:00 AM.

Rick and I had always wanted to visit Europe and had previously traveled extensively throughout the Caribbean, Canada, Mexico, and the United States. In February 2005, Rick learned that he had prostate cancer that was to be treated with hormones and radiation. He opted to start his treatment when we returned from our European vacation. It was no big deal and we were prepared to deal with it upon our return. *We had no idea that this cancer was just the tip of the iceberg.*

Our trip of a lifetime was in May 2005. We went to Europe with Phyllis and Don. We toured London, France, Switzerland, Monaco, and Italy. You name it, we saw it. If I saw it, I bought it! During this trip, I noticed that Rick was shuffling his big ole size 13 feet. He had purchased some new walking shoes with a wider sole than normal. I thought this was why he was shuffling his feet. I said to him, on more than one occasion (trust me), "Good grief, Man, can't you pick up your feet?" Phyllis mentioned that she and Don noticed that Rick had really slowed down a lot. Mmmmm… I thought he just needed to work out more when we got home. "Pump that iron, pump that iron." At this time I had a personal trainer and worked out quite a bit and just "knew" that working out would solve just about *everything*.

Once we got back home, Rick started experiencing a persistent pain in his right leg. We—make that "I"— thought that it was again a lack of exercise or even a degenerative disc due to his sedentary life style. Rick was a big WWII buff and watched anything associated with war and was quite knowledgeable. He went to the chiropractor, the physical therapist, and was on pain medication. Rick also started his 36 radiation treatments for the prostate cancer.

The pain didn't get any better. I watched in horror as he went from using a cane for balance, then a walker and finally to my pushing him in a wheelchair. His medical doctor suggested an MRI and then a bone scan of his L3 vertebra. Both tests were inconclusive but pointed towards a degenerative disc. During this phase, I was on the Internet researching like a mad woman trying to find anything related to his symptoms. I also developed my Chronology of Treatment Matrix, which I will discuss later in more detail.

His wonderful radiation oncologist suggested that we do a CAT scan needle-directed biopsy (ouch). He said there was a slim chance that it might be cancer, but he wanted to rule this out.

But it was cancer. Emergency back surgery was scheduled for Rick. The surgery went well and he was even able to stand on his right leg the day after surgery. His surgeon removed a tumor which had wrapped around and eaten away his L3 vertebra. This tumor was the size of a hockey puck! No wonder the poor man was in so much pain. He had to wear a large plastic vest for three months after the surgery to protect the hardware that was installed once the L3 vertebra was completely removed. He could take the brace off at night or when he was lying in bed. The next step was 10 radiation treatments to the surgical area.

His case was transferred to a medical oncologist. We loved our medical oncologist because he was a no-nonsense kinda guy who told us what was what straight up. He said that Rick's cancers were not related and that the cancer in his back came from somewhere else. Another CAT scan would be required to find out the origin of the tumor and the nature of the treatment..

The day that we were to find out the results of his CAT scan, we both thought independently that if the doctor came into the examination room by himself, the situation wasn't that bad. However, if he came into the room with someone else, it was bad. You don't need two people to tell you good news. Well into the room came our doctor, so I thought, "Cool, this is very cool." Then an intern walked in right behind him. I thought, *"Oh… not good, not good!"* We were told that Rick had Stage 4 lung cancer with six to twelve months to live. ***We were in shock and devastated***. When we got home, Rick said that he wanted some time by himself. I watched as he sadly hobbled to a bench up the street from our home and sat with his head down, resting his chin on the top of his cane.

Chemotherapy was recommended and Rick opted for this type of treatment. Chemo took the very life out of him for the next three months. I did not want him to take the chemotherapy treatments, but wanted him to either try a holistic form of treatment or just roll the dice and let's go and live our lives the best that we can until the very end. In his case, chemo proved to be a thief and a robber. He selected the type of treatment that he wanted and all I could do was to support what he wanted to do. In retrospect, we both said that we should have traveled the three months that he was bedridden and seen many of the sights, particularly the Panama Canal, that he had always wanted to see. It was gut-wrenching to see someone that I deeply cared about lose 100 pounds and just wither away. I could do nothing about it. Tears; ah yes, there were many tears.

As I reviewed my mental tapes after the fact, I can see that the signs of his illness were there long before the official diagnosis. I would get a cold; Rick would get pneumonia or bronchitis. Whatever was going around always seemed to settle in his lungs. I have often wondered if a simple chest x-ray could have caught this cancer before the tumor in his chest grew to the size of a deck of cards. This thought floats in and out of my mind when I reflect on his illness. Maybe, … I just don't know…

Now wait a minute I thought, there ***was*** something that I could and would do!

I have always been an organized fool. My sister, Ellouise, claims that I organized my toys as a child. I decided to use this "personality trait" to help me navigate through this process. While Rick was downstairs in a chemo-based stupor, I was upstairs doing research, documenting and trying to get my arms around what *was* happening to us, what *would* happen to us, and what the next step should be for him.

My daughter, Wendy, was a driving force behind my inception and writing of this book. Whenever I began to doubt myself or my abilities to even write this book, she was a one-woman cheering squad, chanting something like, "You can do it. You can do it. You can do it, IF you try. Go, Mom!" Wendy even kept her cool after editing the first half of my book. My feelings were raw and anything that she said other than it was the most important literary accomplishment ever written by mankind was responded to by two hours of defensive comments on my part. She calmly talked me off the ceiling and said that I needed to toughen up a bit if I wanted to become a serious writer. Wendy said that I had something good going here, but I needed to prepare myself because my editors would definitely give me feedback. I needed to learn to handle any type of feedback. The child is now teaching the parent. A bit of role reversal, don't you think?

Rick died peacefully at home. Our hospice social worker told Rick early in the process that he had an opportunity to teach us how to die, and teach us he did. He handled the entire process with such grace and dignity that it was mind-boggling. Not once did he complain, pity himself, or ask "Why me, Lord?" He once even told me, "Why not me, Bea?"

Thanks to hospice care, he was able to die in the comfort of our home surrounded by family, friends, his Bible and his many books, with the History Channel or Military Channel on in the background. During his final few days on earth, he had a beautiful Native American CD, *Canyon Trilogy*, by R. Carlos Nakai, playing softly in his sick room as he transitioned on to the next life.

He was buried with full military honors and, per his wishes, alongside his other military buddies at the San Joaquin Valley Military Cemetery in Gustine, California. Ironically, the grave next to Rick was of a fallen airman who was born two months before Rick's birthday and died two months before Rick's death.

Rest on, Rick, rest on... You are deeply missed by all who crossed your path.

Oh, Lord, Say It Isn't So!

You ever feel like you have been hit in the face with a shovel? Well that is what it feels like when you have a loved one who has been diagnosed with a catastrophic illness. You will have a thousand million thoughts colliding in your head and may go from being extremely eloquent to sounding like Porky Pig.

They say that there are several distinct stages of dealing with a crisis. Disbelief, Anger, Acceptance and then Moving On. (See *How to Survive the Loss of a Love* by Peter McWilliams, Harold H. Bloomfield, and Melba Colgrove.) From my experience, it ain't that neat and tidy. The first thing that I want you to do as a caregiver is the following:

> *Women: Turn in your Wonder Woman bracelets, belt and shoes.*
> *Fellas: Turn in your Superman cape and tights.*

You cannot handle all aspects of the care of your loved one by yourself. *Reaching out for help is not a sign of weakness.* **There needs to be a new super hero called CAREGIVER.** This hero would have to have wings, eight arms and three pairs of legs… what a visual! Take it from me, being a caregiver is not for sissies; it will be one of the hardest jobs that you will ever do. You will be dog tired and so overwhelmed at times that you will be spinning in circles. There were times that I simply didn't even know where I was or why I was even there.

If you are anything like me, you can allow that nervous energy to work for you and not against as you start to unravel with this added responsibility.

Documentation

"Failing to Plan is Planning to Fail."

First Things First

When I worked for Xerox Corporation in sales, there was an adage that we often used: "Failing to Plan is Planning to Fail." You *have to have a plan* and basic organization in order to traverse this caregiver minefield. You are not alone in this process and there are support systems all around you; you just have to tap into them. Being organized will allow you to maximize your time whenever you have to talk to someone. Organization will actually give you more control over the situation.

Once you have been given some baseline information on your loved one's illness, both of you need to do your homework. In my opinion, a doctor has just a bit more information on my health than I have. I have found that medical professionals respond differently to a patient who seems to be more informed. You will also develop more confidence in handling the illness once you have more information. You will be able to be more conversant, able to better understand what is really going on, and able to ask appropriate second-level questions.

Key items that you will need to start your documentation process are listed below:

An accordion file folder with marked tabs. Suggested tabs are:

- o Medical Record Numbers
- o Matrix
- o Lab Reports
- o Notes and Meetings
- o Business Cards
- o Health Plan Benefits and Requirements
- o Invoices and Bills
- o Reference Material
- o Phone Messages (tape small notes to an 8 x 11 piece of paper)
- o Note Paper
- o Miscellaneous
- o Blank Tabs

Make sure that you have your name and phone number taped or written in permanent ink on the inside of the folder.

A spiral notebook. This is a must. If you don't get anything else, get this right away. If you rely on Post-It Notes, or other bits of paper to write down information, they can become lost in the shuffle or stuck to other documents. Write down phone numbers and other information, MAKING SURE 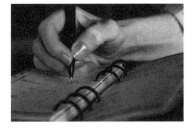 that you date the top of each page for easy reference. If you have information on a Post-It or bit of paper, tape them to a full page in your spiral notebook. When you talk to someone, make sure that you get a number and a name. The actual phone number of the representative or his or her extension number or secretary's name is always best so that you won't be caught up in an evil voice-mail loop.

PLEASE write your name and phone number in this book in the event that you leave it somewhere. For instance, I had an appointment at Kaiser and I accidentally left my Bible, but not my notebook behind. However, since my name and phone number was in the Bible,

Kaiser called me to let me know that they had it. I was so frazzled that I didn't even know I had left it behind. Whew!

Also, on a regular basis, I would review my spiral notebook and check off an item with a highlighter to indicate that I have completed a task. I would use a small colorful Post-It on the edge of a page if there was a task that needed follow-up or hadn't been done. Again, once you start doing this, it will become second nature to you, and you will remain on top of the tasks at hand.

Pen, pencil, red pen/pencil and a highlighter
Business Cards

> *Yes, Business Cards*. You will be surprised how often you will need them. Even if you are retired, you need business cards... retirement and caregiving for a loved one is NOW your business. A great place to get them printed for a nominal cost is <u>vistaprint.com</u>. You just pay for shipping and they will send you the cards.

Keep all of these items together in the accordion file folder.

This seems like a simple concept, but is one that will assist you in keeping yourself together. You will be surprised by the amount of paperwork that will suddenly appear as you go through a health crisis. It will help keep your cool when you are asked for information, which then is readily available at your fingertips. Yes, I am repeating myself.

Be vigilant about your use of this process and *make sure that you have your business cards or your name and phone number on the folder,* in the event, heaven help you, you should either lose or misplace it.

Calendar

As the nature of an illness or disability progresses, you will be tasked with coordinating a myriad of appointments, consultations, meetings, and personal appointments. Some type of a calendar is a must. Blackberry or Palm Pilot-like electronic devices are great, **IF** you are disciplined to use them and they don't crash on you. If there are several people that need access to this information, I would suggest a computer-generated calendar that you can create on a regular basis and post it in key spots. You can download these calendars from multiple sites on the Internet and fill them in on an on-going basis.

I found that I needed to actually see what was scheduled. I kept one copy on the refrigerator and one at Rick's bedside. This allowed Rick to know what was going on and he could help coordinate any additional appointments or activities. Another copy of the calendar was kept on a bulletin board in my dressing area. At night, when I was brushing my teeth or applying face cream— or heaven forbid actually flossing my teeth— I could look at the calendar and see what I had going on the next day or two. I also kept a planner with me when I went to various appointments. Any new information would be transferred to my computerized calendar when I got home. As a result, I was able to coordinate the plethora (I love that word) of appointments required to deal with Rick's cancer and my other personal obligations. This sounds like a lot of work, but once you get in the groove, it is not. Even with this process, you will find that you will drop a few balls along the way. The calendarizing will minimize the number of balls dropped. In just a few days, this will become second nature to you.

An added benefit was that LaCressia, the in-home health care professional who took care of Rick, would review the calendar on the refrigerator. On several occasions, she would remind me of an impending appointment, if it looked like I was buzzing around the house and not moving out the door in a timely manner.

If you don't want to type it out, just use one of the free calendars that you can pick up at the beginning of the year or go to your local stationery store. A large desk size calendar would be ideal if you had a central location to post it. The key is to make sure that you use a pencil and have a calendar that is large enough to post the information. A colored pen or pencil and highlighter will work wonders in keeping your ever-growing schedule intact. At the end of each day, I would cross off that day's action items and then look forward a couple of days to see what I was expected to juggle during the week.

Also, clip business cards or appointment cards on this wall calendar or keep them in the physical calendar that you actually carry to your appointments. A couple of systems may have to be tried until you find out which one is most effective.

Post-It Notes are also a good idea to jot down a quick note or thought. However, they can stick to something else and goodness knows where they will end up. If I opted to use a Post-It, I would try to remember to transfer that information onto my calendar or into my spiral notebook. Try to keep your spiral notebook on your nightstand and take it around the house with you during the day. If you find yourself still using the Post-Its, consider dating them and taping them inside the spiral notebook.

Here is a sample of one of my real-life calendar. NOTE: Although there is a 7:30 PM Salsa class listed on my calendar... I have yet to attend a class. It is a goal, an unrealized goal, but still a goal.

March 2006

Sunday	Monday	Tuesday	Wednesday	Thursday	Friday	Saturday
Contact Surgeon's Office for follow-up appointment **Dr. ___ (916) 784-___**			1 11:00 AM Carla, Hair Appt. 3:00 PM Alex, MSW	2	3 12:30 PM Ellen, Chaplain	4 Grandkid's Ball Game
5 Sunday School	6 9:30 AM Visiting Angels 1:30 PM Morgan and Jones Pre-Need Funeral Arrangements	7 Visiting Deacons Communion at Home 7:30 PM Salsa Class	8 Ladelle's BD 11:30 AM Jefferson's Luncheon 1:30 PM Ardys, Nurse 3:00 PM Alex, MSW	9 8:00 AM Jake, Trainer 10:00 AM – 2:00 PM Visiting Angels	10 8:00 AM to 3:00 PM Bea to Proctor EXAM Aubrey is taking Rick to Lunch	11 Ruth and Larry to play cards @3:00 PM
12 Sunday School	13 10:00 AM – 2:00 PM Visiting Angels	14 8:00 AM Jake, Trainer 7:30 PM Salsa Class	15 9:15 AM (Rick) Podiatry Morse Ave 11:00 AM – 3:00 PM Visiting Angels	16 8:00 AM Jake, Trainer	17 10:00 AM – 2:00 PM Visiting Angels	18

The Matrix

The **Spiral Notebook** that I have previously discussed and the **Chronology of Treatment Matrix** I am about to discuss are the key documents you should use to track the treatment of your loved one or yourself.

When I worked for Xerox and then the State of California, I was responsible for keeping track of a lot of data. My software of choice was Microsoft Excel. You can sort your data in a variety of ways and add color and impact. Whenever I met with a medical professional, I would document what occurred. Doing this kept everyone on the same page. Some of the advantages of using the matrix are that it will:

☐ **Help keep you on track**. You are entering an information overload period and this will be your medical treatment road map. You should not and will not be able to rely on your recall of medical details.

☐ Provide detailed information for **future medical personnel**, particularly if you have to change doctors, have a multitude of doctors or healthcare professionals.

☐ **Increase** your **level of confidence** and **calm your nerves**. You will have key information at your fingertips and eliminate a lot of needless fumbling and associated frustration.

☐ Provide the basis for a **potential lawsuit**. If you have received inferior or inappropriate medical treatment, you will have the facts and timelines already documented.

I have a friend who is currently navigating through a series of medical issues. I had previously shown her my matrix and she is now using it. It has helped her tremendously in her efforts to get to the bottom of her health issues by having a specific timeline and chronology of treatment.

This matrix should be updated on a weekly or bi-weekly basis. Make sure that you leave some blank spaces at the end of your current matrix so that you can handwrite in new information and type it in later.

If the computer is not your cup of tea, you can also do this by hand. You could use a separate spiral notebook for this task. Again, please label it and include your name and phone number in this notebook.

Knowledge is Power. Trust me, this concept works.

Here is a sample of Rick's matrix. By the time that Rick died, our matrix was over 25 pages long. The following form is portrait; I preferred the landscape format when I completed Rick's matrix. However, it is a matter of personal preference.

Name: Richard J. Bailey
Medical Record Number: XXXXXXXXXX

CHRONOLOGY OF TREATMENT MATRIX

Date	Provider Phone Number	Issue	Treatment	Status
1/27/05	Dr. _____ (916) 973-_____	Biopsy of Prostrate performed	Rick went on his own to do this procedure. It wasn't particularly difficult	
2/1/05	Dr. _____ (916) 973-_____	Diagnosed with Prostate Cancer.	Hormone Shots and Radiation recommended. Given the first of three 4-Month Hormone Shots	
5/1/05	Dr. _____ (916) 723-_____	Severe back pain	Started chiropractic adjustments. 5/4/05, 5/9/05, 5/16/05, 5/18/05	
May 22-June 5, 2005		Toured Europe for 17 days and back pain and significant shuffling of his feet started.		
6/29/05	Dr. _____ (916) 973-_____	Started the daily radiation	Oncology Department	
7/6/05	Dr. _____ (916) 973-_____	Back pain has continued	MRI conducted Oncology Department	
7/1/05, 7/8/05, 7/22/05	PT @ (916) 614-_____	Trying other options	Physical Therapy	Another appointment is scheduled 8/4/05
7/29/05	Dr. _____ (916) 973-_____	Richard given a prescription for morphine	Both Richard and Wife are alarmed by this.	We want the matter addressed and not simply covered up with medication.
7/29/05	Dr. _____ (916) 973-_____	Another pain medication prescribed	Dr.'s office has ordered a prescription for a stronger Vicoden	Bea to pick it up on 7/30/05

DOCUMENTATION
Action Items

Done (X)	Item	Required Action	Status	Comments

Meeting with the Healthcare Professionals

Why Ask Why?

Dig in and do your homework. Once you are given an initial diagnosis, you need to do a full court press in order to get as much information as you can about the illness or disease. Key areas where you can obtain baseline information are:

☐ **The Internet**

The Internet is a wealth of information for almost anything you want to know. Use one of the search engines (ie. Yahoo or Goggle) to find information for all topics that interest you. For instance, if you're looking for information about cancer treatment for melanoma, you might want to type in "key words", such as "cancer" or "melanoma" or "treatment". You will then be provided with links on that topic and related areas. An excellent site that was recommended to me was webmd.com

☐ **Library**

The local public library has an impressive catalogue of books to arm you with information. In addition, the library also has Internet access for free. You can do your research and just pay for the copies you print.

☐ **Other Medical Personnel**

Don't be afraid to ask one of your other trusted doctors his or her opinion about what is going on with you or your loved one. Even though your loved one's illness may not be the physician's specialty, you may get verification of what is going on or a completely different take on the matter.

□ **Second Opinion**

This is your right. If you just don't feel comfortable with your relationship with the doctor or what he or she is telling you, you can ask for another opinion. This can come either from that same medical organization or you can strike out on your own. You could contact another segment of this medical organization or an entity completely outside of this organization. However, you need to find out what the associated charges are for this second opinion. Getting a second opinion is your right and you don't have to feel that you are slighting your doctor. Your allegiance is to your loved one and yourself.

I once had a doctor who had a reputation of being the best of the best. He was the "Doctor's Doctor." Well… he was good and very thorough, but had one of the WORST bedside manners I ever encountered. He was such a put-down artist that I found excuses for not going to see him when I was ill. Needless to say, I asked for another doctor. He just wasn't a good fit for me. I kept inquiring about other options and am pleased with my current doctor.

□ **Ask Around**

This might be a bit touchy. You might get too much information and it might be all over the map. Select a few trusted and knowledgeable people and pick their brains. Someone who has actually gone through what you and your family are going through might be a good place to start.

You make the final call. Note that you will have to develop a filter to sift through a lot of information, but it will be a beginning. You will feel empowered with this new body of knowledge. As a result, you will be able to develop more informed questions.

☐ **Questions and Preparation**

Rick was more comfortable with me taking the lead in handling many aspects of his healthcare. As a result, I always came to any medical meeting with at least three questions for the doctor or therapist.

Samples of questions that you could pose are:

What is the diagnosis?

How long has he/she had this condition?

How rare is it?

Where can I find other information on this issue?

Where could be get a second opinion?

Is it hereditary?

What are our options?

What if we did nothing at this time?

What are our next steps?

These questions will become more detailed as you begin to fully understand the illness or disability you are facing and as other associated variables of the illness begin to unfold.

Type or write your questions out, leaving space to write in your answers. Keep this in your accordion folder under a tab marked "Notes and Meetings."

Questions for Back Surgeon
Month/Date/Year
4:00 PM

1) Location of hospital

2) Time of surgery

3) Length of surgery

4) Nature of surgery

5) Will he go to a nursing home for rehabilitation?

Here is a sample of what I took with me to our first meeting with Rick's doctor on his diagnosis of prostate cancer:

Meeting with Proctologist
Month/Date/Year
10:30 AM

Questions Regarding Prostate Cancer

1.   Stages

2.   Recommended treatment

3.   Effectiveness of treatment

4.   What if we opt not to have this type of treatment?

5.   Sexual side effects?

6.   Weight gain and appetite issues?

7.   Recovery rate in view of manageable diabetes

8.   Next step?

9.   What are the odds of Rick being ready to take a trip to Europe at the end of May?

10.   How soon can he start working out and walking?

See, I just had to get that exercise thing in, didn't I?

11.   Do diet and exercise play a part in developing prostate cancer?

12.   Are there any diet restrictions during his recovery period and treatment?

I left plenty of room on these forms when I typed them out so that I could write down the answers from the doctor. When we got home, if we had any additional questions, I would go to the Internet for more background information. If I still wasn't satisfied, we would then make a follow-up appointment with the doctor or give him/her a call.

You could create a separate form for these meeting, however, I opted to either use my spiral notebook or type them on separate sheets of paper. After the meetings, I would file these questions and answers in my accordion folder.

MEETING WITH HEALTHCARE PROFESSIONALS
Action Items

Done (X)	Item	Required Action	Status	Comments

Organization and Time Savers

*"There cannot be a crisis next week.
My schedule is already full."*

—Henry Kissinger

Setting up the Sick Room

When you are faced with a long-term illness, you will have to decide which area of your home is the most convenient for both your patient and you. The location of your sick room and how you set it up are essential to effectively caring for your patient.

Originally, Rick was upstairs on the second floor in his den on his favorite couch, where the BIG television was located. Well guess what? When he wanted something to eat, I had to run downstairs, get it, and come back upstairs. Oops, he wanted hot sauce … down I went again. Oops, he also wanted a pickle. You get my point. It became clear just before his back surgery that it would be more efficient to set up the *downstairs* living room as the sick room. It was right off the kitchen and there was a powder room on the first floor. Rick was able to receive his many visitors downstairs and they would not have to trek upstairs to see him. This eliminated the stress of keeping the entire house squeaky clean and orderly at all times. Making this change saved me a lot of wear and tear and made everything far more convenient.

Rick and I worked with Carol, a social worker, who was assigned to the Kaiser Oncology Department. We met with her on the morning that Rick found out that he had cancer on his

L3 vertebra and would be having emergency surgery that week. Carol hopped on this situation immediately, and that same evening a hospital bed, with a trapeze, bedside table, walker, bedside commode and wheelchair were delivered to our home. This made a world of difference for both of us and Rick was able to recuperate from surgery in comfort. Now is a good time to find out from your medical plan coordinator if there are costs associated with obtaining this type of equipment and any related timeframes for keeping it.

Rearrange the furniture so that the room is inviting and will accommodate at least two visitors. You will be surprised at how creative you can be. I moved our sectional to another side of the room and I actually like it there much better than the original location. When Rick's sister, Barbara and her son Mitch came to play cards and to see Rick, the rearranged room just was perfect for this visit.

Other Suggestions for Managing the Sick Room:

- ☐ **Containerize key items**. Doing this will keep down the visual "noise" in a sick room. You don't have to spend a fortune doing this. You can cruise on down to the local dollar store and find a nice variety of containers.
  - o Place all **toiletries** in one bin and place in the bathroom.
  - o Use one of these bins to hold all of your patient's **prescription and non-prescription medicine**. I also had the "List of Medication Matrix" in this bin so that I would know exactly how to restock his pill boxes.
  - o Put **hand towels** or **washcloths** on the back of the toilet tank or under the sink. If there isn't a toilet nearby, I would use a bin or basket that contained these items for easy access.
  - o Add a **nightstand or plastic stand with drawers** where you can store underwear, change of pajamas, etc.
  - o Rearrange a nearby **bookcase** so that you can place some of the items mentioned here on selected shelves.
  - o Purchase a **green plant or flowers** to make the room as attractive as possible. I purchased variegated ivy which was not only lovely to look at but required minimal maintenance.

- Place **writing instruments** and paper nearby for easy access for both your patient and you.

- Get **extension cords** so that you can plug in a fan to freshen up the room or to recharge a cell phone, etc.

- Dig out any **travel mugs** that you have lying around. If you or your patient are taking pain medications, these medications might make you a bit "loopy" and downright clumsy. Your day will not start off on a good note, if you happen to come downstairs and find two cups of black coffee spilled on your blond carpet. I found that fewer mishaps occurred when I had Rick use this type of container.

  > **Hint:** If you have a _light carpet_ and there is a coffee or cola stain in it, follow the directions and spray the area with some sort of standard cleaner. If the stain persists, put some hydrogen peroxide in a squirt bottle and lightly spray the area. I tried it on my blond carpeting and it worked like a charm, but I tried a test area first to make sure that this application worked. I strongly suggest that you do the same if you are opting to try this household hint. The best is to call in a professional carpet cleaner.

- I would have plenty of **bottled water** on hand and made sure that Rick had at least two bottles at his bedside at all times. You can also put juice or lemonade or other liquids in them for convenience.

- Have **an extra set of bed sheets** nearby. If you are using a hospital bed, you will need twin, extra long sheets and mattress pads. Also consider having both a heavy and a light-weight comforter and spread available.

- Keep a **large bath towel** neatly folded and readily available.

- Put up some **TV trays** in key locations. I had one near where the visitors sat and one off to the side of his bed for items that he needed but didn't use every day. I purchased a **hospital bedside table** because it was less expensive in the long run. It could be raised or lowered based upon Rick's needs. Afterwards, it was perfect for my painting supplies.

- **Garage Door Opener**. Yes, I said garage door opener. I taped an extra one on the side of his bedside table. If I was not home and he was expecting a visitor, all he had to do was to push the opener and let his guests in for a visit. This allowed him control of the situation and maximum security. Rick, who was very security conscious, could sleep soundly knowing that the house was locked up and secure.

- **Air out the room daily**, if you can. I would open up the front door and the door to the laundry room for about a half an hour. Make sure your patient is covered up and nice and warm. There is something very invigorating about fresh air coursing through a sick room. Now, don't freeze the poor patient. Depending on the weather, you might be able to do this for only a few minutes.

- **Purchase some plastic runners** from your hardware store. Place these in the high traffic areas of the sick room. I had a long one that ran from the entrance of the living room up to his bed. Another one ran along the other side of the bed. I then placed carpet runners in different locations to add color and to handle the foot traffic. Some of these runners have perforated sections and may separate a bit. **A note of caution:** make sure that these runners are firmly fixed to the floor and are not a hazard that could cause someone to trip. I used reinforced tape to anchor the corners so that no one broke their dat gum neck

- **A bell or other communication device** is important, particularly if you have a two-story house. You can purchase a simple intercom system or use a baby monitor. Even the use of a bell will make the patient feel more in control. Of course, the OVER use of the bell might result in you taking the little clapper OUT of the bell and tossing it out the window. Rick and I would use our cell phones to call each other. If I was upstairs and didn't want to yell or come downstairs, I'd call him on his cell phone.

- **Type out a list of all medications.** This list should include the prescription number, dosage, etc. I kept an extra copy with the folder I took to the doctor, his chemo appointments, other medical appointments, etc. I also had a copy inside the hospice binder in his sick room for easy reference. Here is a sample of the form that I used:

Name: Richard J. Bailey
Medical Record Number: XXXXXXXXXXX

LIST OF MEDICATIONS

Medication Prescription Non-Prescription	RX#	Unit	Dosage	Frequency	Comments
Dexamethsone	RX#	4 Mg	2 Tablets	Before bedtime when taking Taxatere	Prevent Inflammation
Dolasteron	RX#	100 MG	1 Tablet	Daily	Nausea
Iron	Over the Counter	65 Mg	1 Tablet	Daily	Help with Red Blood Count
Actos	RX#	15 Mg	2 Tablets	Daily	Help with Processing Insulin
Insulin	N: R:		In AM: 18N 10 R In PM 10R or 5R for every 100 pts.	10N AM Only	Diabetes
Hydrocodone Acetaminophen For Norco (Vicoden)	RX#	10/325	1 Tablet	Every 6 Hours	Break through pain
Dexamethsone	RX#	4 Mg	2 Tablets	Before bedtime when taking Taxatere	Prevent Inflammation
Dolasteron	RX#	100 MG	1 Tablet	Daily	Nausea
Benedryl	RX#	25Mg	1-2 Tablets	As Needed	Sleep Aid & Anxiety
Calcium	Over the Counter	Vitamin D 200 IU Calcium 500 Mg Sodium 5 Mg	2 Tablets	(1) AM (1) PM	Dietary Supplement

☐ **Daily pill containers**: These containers can be picked up anywhere. I purchased one that I really liked at the Dollar Store. Use the above form to set up the daily medications for a week. If you purchase two containers, you can do two weeks at a time.

   o **Hint**: When you are down to only two weeks of medication, reorder right away so that you don't run out of your supply. Some medications have to be reordered when you have actually run out of the medicine. Please note: If your loved one is under hospice care, even over-the-counter medications may be free of charge, if they are part of the patient's plan of treatment. Check with your medical plan(s) for any prescription costs, if you are referred to hospice. Most plans waive associated fees for hospice patients.

- **Small 1 oz. paper cups** are great to use to dispense the AM and/or PM medications. It results in dispensing the medicine in an organized and sanitary manner.

- **Portable Urinals** are extremely useful for both your patient and you. Try pouring about one-eighth of a cup of disinfectant into the urinal to keep it smelling fresh. This also can be used in the standing commodes that you received from the hospital or purchase at a medical supply store.

- **Program key phone numbers** into both your cell phone(s) and home phone(s). You will be calling these numbers on a regular basis and it is just one less step that you have to take.

- **Daily diary**: I didn't start using a daily diary until the last few months of Rick's illness. I thought that I was on top of what he was eating and his blood sugar readings (he was a diabetic), but when the nurse would ask me second or third level questions, I didn't have a clue. He once told the nurse that he had bacon and eggs and toast for breakfast. I was listening to the call and thought "Ahh... unless he got up from his sick bed and cooked breakfast himself, I knew that I certainly didn't cook them." So I purchased a medium size spiral notebook and used this to log in information on his daily activities. Some of the suggested headings are:
  - Date
  - Time he woke up
  - Blood Sugar Reading
  - Amount of Insulin Used
  - AM Medications
  - PM Medications
  - Bowel Movement
  - Bath
  - What he ate for breakfast, lunch, dinner, snacks and any beverages
  - Activity Level
  - Notes and Comments: i.e., appetite, sleeping habits during the day and any other issues about which the nurse might want to know.

Here is a sample of the format that I used to capture this daily information.

Daily Diary

Woke Up:_____
Urine Output:
Blood Sugar Reading:
____Units of "N"
____Units of "R"
____AM Meds
____PM Meds
Bath ___Yes ____No
BM ___Yes ____No

```
+-----------------------------+
|        Vital Signs          |
|                             |
| Blood Pressure:             |
| _____                    |
| Temperature:                |
| _____                    |
| Pulse:                      |
| _____            |
+-----------------------------+
```

Meals

Breakfast	Lunch	Dinner	Snacks

Activity Level:

_____
_____
_____

Comments:

_____
_____
_____
_____

Once the in-home aides started coming on a regular basis, I instructed them how to make the entries. Whenever the hospice nurse would come to visit, she would thumb through this notebook and was immediately up-to-date on the status of Rick's behavior and activities during the previous week. It was extremely helpful to the nurse for her evaluating any trends or corrections that needed to take place in Rick's treatment plan. The nurse would review each day's activities since her last visit. I would put a Post-It in the diary with any message or questions on Rick's previous week's activities for the nurse to review during her next scheduled home visit.

An additional benefit was that the diary helped to resolve a billing dispute between two aides who worked for us on a particular day. The notes in the diary reflected which aide actually worked on the day in question. When I produced the daily diary with the correct aide's entries, the billing dispute was resolved.

Selecting the Personnel

This is one of the most important decisions that you will have to make. It is imperative that you select someone who is a good fit for your loved one and yourself. We were blessed to have LaCressia, of Visiting Angels, and our niece, Monique, each of whom were ideal for Rick. They were very attentive to his needs, quiet, respectful and trustworthy. They gave him phenomenal back and foot rubs and were kind to both of us. You might initially have an aide that is very efficient but too high energy or too emotionally absent from the care giving process. If there are any issues or concerns, please work with your in-home care service coordinator to resolved them. You might have to employ a couple of different people before you find the correct fit. If not, you will be doing both your loved one and yourself a disservice. *The point is to do whatever it takes to minimize any tension in the house.*

List of Key Contacts

I kept a list of key contacts on the backside of the same clear protective sheet that held the computerized calendar and kept these documents by Rick's bedside. I also had a list in plain view on the refrigerator. Here is a sample of what I used:

Richard Bailey
Medical Record #XXXXXXXXXXX
HEALTHCARE
CONTACTS

Name	Relationship to Patient	Phone Numbers Home, Work, Cell	Comments
Bea	Wife	Cell and Home Phone #s	
	Hospice Nursing Supervisor		
	Hospice Nurse, Social Worker		
	Chaplain, Your Pastor or other Religious Leader		
	Children		
	Key Friends		
There may be multiple personnel	Home Health Aides	Get the cell number, if available	
	Hospice Volunteer or Friend		
	Emergency Contact (I would suggest a couple of names)		

Coordinating Help

This proved to be a challenge. There were friends, neighbors and hospice workers who were coming in on a regular basis to assist us. Once we added the long-term healthcare personnel, scheduling was less of a challenge.

In order to keep things running smoothly in the home, I created a document of action items for homecare providers. This document clarified the care that Rick required. It also allowed me the freedom to run errands outside of the house without worrying about Rick's care.

HOME HEALTH CARE
ACTION ITEMS

Action Item	Description	Comments
Dressing	Please help him get dressed.	
	Lotion his legs and arms	
	Check his blood sugar levels. He can do this himself, however.	
Activities	Encourage him to move around and stay up more. We are trying to extend the length of time between his doses of medicine.	
	Massage his feet	He really likes this and it promotes his circulation.
	Exercises	Make sure that he does them. He also should take a walk outside. I would encourage him to use his walker and I would like for you to walk with him around the cul-de-sac. This should be done a couple of times. He needs to build up his endurance.
Meals	Lunch	He might like a ham sandwich
Medical	Make an appointment with Podiatry Please call Roseville Podiatry @ 784-XXXX and make an appointment for his pedicure. I am available on the days highlighted on the attached calendar.	Rick's Kaiser # is XXXXXX. You can state that there have been no changes to any phone numbers or addresses when they ask you these questions.

Periodic respite is essential for caregivers. When I opted to take time out to rest and recuperate, I created a matrix that I gave to the people who were caring for Rick. It had all of the pertinent information on it, and everyone knew how to contact each other.

Here is my sample matrix:

Name: Richard Bailey
Medical Record Number: XXXX

RESPITE CALENDAR

Date	12:00 –6:00 AM	6:00 – 9:00 AM	9:00-5:00 AM/PM	5:00-12:00 PM/AM	Comments
10/5/05	Bea	Cindy	Mary	Monique	
10/6/05	Sister	Cindy	Mary	Monique	Shift Change
10/7/05	Sister	Cindy	Mary		Bea Returns Home@ 7:00 PM

Make sure that you leave your cell phone number and the number of the location where you are staying.

Volunteer Agencies

There are many agencies available that can assist you in providing transportation and related services. There is excellent information on services provided on the American Cancer Society web site, (www.cancer.org) and American Diabetes Society web site (www.Diabetes.org) for similar information.

If you are a member of a church, synagogue, temple, or lodge you should also contact the administrative office to find out if there are volunteers available to assist you and your family.

Handling Phone Messages

You may be inundated by phone calls from many well-wishers. There may also be several return calls from attorneys, medical professionals, or family members. When you return home from a medical appointment, short trip, or a hospital visit, there may be multiple calls on your answering machine. People mean well and want to find out what is happening because they care. Of course, there are some people who are just down right nosey. However, dispensing this information and responding to the multiple calls will ultimately wear you out in no time.

Here is a simple way to handle this situation:

- ☐ On your answering machine (if you don't have one, then get one) or phone service voice mail, **leave an updated message** for those who call. You can be as brief or as detailed as you want. When I did this, I found that my daily calls went from ten per day to only about two. Two calls is far more manageable than ten. Also be really selective about to whom you give your cell phone number. Not only can the calls wear you out, they may ultimately impact your monthly phone usage. All you would now need is to have a gigantic cell phone overage bill to push you over the top.

- ☐ Purchase **a phone message book** with carbonless paper from your local stationery store. This book allows you to write down the call, tear out the message, and still have a backup record of who has called you. Do not rely on your memory at this time. This is an excellent aid for anyone who is answering the phone for you while you are busy with your patient or not at home.

- ☐ **Program Key Numbers into your cell phone or home phone**. You will be calling your doctors, pharmacy, or hospice on a regular basis. With these numbers programmed into your cell phone, you have constant access to these numbers. You can call them when needed, except of course when you are driving in the car ("wink, wink").

The following are some hints to help you lighten your load around the house. There are a lot of books and articles along these same lines. I suggest that you get a few books or magazines or use the Internet to further research this area. An excellent web site that I have found is: http://www.realsimple.com. There are interesting suggestions on this website. Also, ask your friends, people at work or other caregivers about ideas that they use to save time and to help organize their households. Something that they might do in passing might be the key to one of your current issues or problems. You will be pleasantly surprised at the number of suggestions you will receive.

Chemotherapy or Radiation Treatment Bag

If your loved one is having either chemo or radiation treatments, they will be on a regular basis. I put together a treatment bag for both Rick and me and took it to each appointment.

Suggested items to include in the bag are:

- ☐ Appointment Information
- ☐ Lab Report
  - o Current Lab Report
  - o Previous Lab Reports
  - o *Future* Blood Work Slips for the laboratory
- ☐ Current Chronology of Treatment Matrix
- ☐ Current List of Medication Matrix
- ☐ Current Key Contact List
- ☐ List of Questions for Doctors
- ☐ Reading material for both you and your loved one
- ☐ Snacks – Note: Only the patient receives juice or crackers during treatment.
- ☐ Box of Tissue
- ☐ A Sweater or Jacket and Long pants – it is very cold in these rooms.
- ☐ Name Tag for your travel bag in the event that you leave it somewhere.

Make sure that you date any documents to ensure that you are working with the most current document.

Food

- ☐ Go to the Dollar Store and get some of those **ceramic dishes** that have plastic covers. I have found them to be ideal to divide up your meals and then freeze. The amount that these containers hold is ideal and can go from the freezer to the microwave if necessary. I would usually take them out of

the freezer the night before and place them in the refrigerator for the next day's meal.

- I have also found that if you use **Romaine lettuce** as a base for your salad, it will last "forever" or at least for a week. I would make a large salad and use the grape tomatoes verses sliced tomatoes. If you slice regular tomatoes or cut up cucumber, these items turn into mush really quickly and you have a mess on your hands.

- **Frozen entrees.** (I won't tell, if you won't tell.) Keep some of these entrees on hand for a quick meal when you don't want to cook or your patient doesn't have much of an appetite.

- Hey, if the patient wants **fast food**, then head to McDonalds or KFC. You just want your loved one to be comfortable, and sometimes fast food is just what the doctor or the caregiver ordered.

- **Individual** Jell-O or pudding **servings** should be made and placed into small plastic containers with lids. I was married to Rick for nine years before I figured out that it was more efficient to use the smaller containers instead of one large one. Rick once told me that as child he was afraid of Jell-O because it moved when he ate it. It that cute or what?

- **Snacks in Zip Lock Bags** are also great. For example, I would purchase a bunch of grapes or melons and divide them into individual serving sizes and place them in the refrigerator. It was really easy for Rick, when he was able to walk, to simply go into the kitchen, reach in the refrigerator, grab a bag of fruit and be on his way. This simple task added to his sense of independence.

Visitors

Handling the amount of traffic in your home can be controlled by you. There are some people whose visits will always be welcomed. However, there are some whom you will want to control. I would set up visiting hours and stick to them. You might have to tell some of the friends who are

visiting with ***each other*** that your patient is getting tired and you would like for them to cut their visit short. Smile sweetly and tell them that you know that they understand, walk them to the door and say ... "Bye, bye."

Also, feel free to place a **Do Not Disturb** sign on your front door. Unplug the phone, blacken the windows or whatever you need to do to allow your loved one and *YOU* get some rest and to have more control over the amount of visits.

Since your loved one might look a bit "scary" because they have been in bed a lot, make sure that you freshen them up a bit. They will look and feel better and their visit will be far more pleasant for all concerned.

The following are some tips that have served me well over the years:

Organization and Time Savers

CATEGORY	TIP
Financial	Have your monthly bills set up on automatic payments through your bank. It is usually free and will save you a lot of time. Even for utility bills that are due every other month, you simply divide the payment in half and have that amount sent each month. Remember that you can always pay more because you will continue to receive your monthly statements. This is a real time saver and will prevent you from getting any overdue notices or a "nastygram" from a creditor.
Financial	Set up a personal ATM at your home. You can use a 5 x 11 accordion folder or just an envelope. Put a series of $20.00 bills (in keeping with your monthly budget) that you can access instead of running to the ATM. This will save time and is much safer than going to the bank ATM early in the AM or late at night.
Housekeeping	No Bleach? Soak your white clothes in hot soap and water the night before. In the AM, turn on the machine and wash as normal. Everything will come out nice and bright.
Meal Preparation	Frozen Chicken Breasts ... yes frozen chicken breast. I stumbled across this quite by accident when I forgot to take some out earlier in the day. Take your boneless skinless chicken breast out of the freezer and season them. Put them directly into a 350 degree oven and bake for about 30 +/ minutes. As the chicken thaws, the juices will keep it unbelievably tender. I then turn the oven to "broil" for a few minutes to brown the breast, make a tossed salad and some rice while it is cooking and then chow down. Any leftover chicken can be used for salad, tacos, etc.
Housekeeping	Fold your clothes immediately when the dryer stops. This will prevent wrinkles and any ironing. Some people still iron, you know.

CATEGORY	TIP
Organization	Keep the personal address labels that you have or receive in the mail in your wallet or readily available. You will be surprised how convenient these are in a pinch.
Organization	Buy birthday and other all occasion cards on sale or at 99 cent stores. Keep them at home and at your office. You will always be able to respond in a timely manner because you have these cards on hand. This is particularly true for Thank You cards. If you are as fortunate as we were, you have the opportunity to send out a lot of these. Also make sure that you have plenty of stamps on hand.
Organization	Children's clothing--buy the same type of white socks with no specific designs on them. This makes it pretty easy to match up socks after washing them. I detest folding socks and this is just one of my pet peeves.
Organization	I have put together a Gift Bin in my guest closet. All throughout the year, I purchase different gifts for kids, adults, babies, teenagers, etc. I get them on sale and try to buy things that have good value. When you are in a time crunch, all you have to do is cruise over to your Gift Bin and select an appropriate gift. I also keep plenty of gift bags and wrapping paper on hand.
Inspirational Reading Material	Keep your Bible with you, at least a small one. You would be surprised how many little bits of time you can find during the day to read a verse or two. I always take my Bible to the beauty shop and to the doctor's office. What a wonderful way to maximize your time. This, of course, works for any other type of literature. I have found that I don't mind waiting, if I have something to do. Try to find something uplifting and inspirational to read. I found that this helped me a lot to keep a more positive mental attitude during Rick's illness.
Spiritual Life	Pray or meditate. You must try to find a bit of time to be still and quiet. Even just lying down and allowing your mind to clear out is a good option. Find a quiet oasis that you can steal away to for a brief portion of the day.
E-mail	Please keep an eye on the amount of e-mail that you are trying to process. I found that I just blew up the ones that asked me to pass them on if I loved Jesus. He knows I love him and he existed and did pretty well getting his message across WITHOUT chain letters. When you receive jokes and other "fluffy" messages, pick and choose them or you will find that you are wasting precious time reading them.
Standard Mail	Do you really need to read all of that junk mail? I take nothing upstairs to my office unless it is a document that I need to read. This would be a bill, wedding, baby or graduation announcement, or a financial paper that I need to file. When you get the mail, go through it in the kitchen and toss the madness. Make sure that if you have any of the promotional checks that come in the mail or anything with your name on it, that you SHRED them immediately. The last thing that you need right now is to have to deal with identity theft.
Organization	I was visiting Phyllis during a recent respite from my caregiver duties and she asked me how I placed my silverware in the dishwasher. She said that she read about one woman would presort the knives, forks, etc. as she loaded up the dishwasher. Bingo, when they were clean, she would just grab like items and put them away. It is also far more sanitary to do it this way.

Disabled Department of Motor Vehicle (DMV) Placard

This was a life saver. You can apply for a **Temporary** or **Permanent Disabled Personal Parking Permit**. You can download a form from your local motor vehicle web site. Take this to your doctor and he/she will fill out the doctor's portion of this application. There is a nominal fee to apply for a temporary placard and no fee in the State of California for a permanent placard. This amount may vary from state to state. Please note that this permit is to be used only when the patient is in the car. It is not a free parking pass for someone who is not disabled.

You will find this will help you as you and your patient go to your many doctor appointments or run to the market, etc. It will also make you keenly aware of the fact that there are a lot of temporary (red placard) and permanently (blue placard) disabled people in the world. When you find that you no longer need this placard, you have return it to the motor vehicle department.

You have been given just a few examples in this section on the ways that you can ease the wear and tear on your family and you. If you are used to having things nice and tidy, you will have to relax your level of order during this time period. I am a bit of a neatnik— no, make that a clean freak— at times. I just had to put that side of myself on the shelf and deal with what was more important— taking care of my husband. You HAVE to learn to not sweat the small stuff, because it really is all small stuff in the overall scheme of things.

Are you sick of me yet? I really did use these tips and as a result I was able to maximize my time. Don't be hard on yourself and learn to relax your standards during this time. Hey, if friends want to come over and vacuum or dust, let them! Wave the white flag; there is help out there for you to ***simplify your life.*** You can be Martha Stewart or B. Smith when your life is less complicated.

ORGANIZATION AND TIME SAVERS
ACTION ITEMS

Done (X)	Item	Required Action	Status	Comments

Name: _____
Medical Record Number: _____
Chronology of Treatment Matrix

Date	Provider Phone Number	Issue	Treatment	Status

SICKROOM CHECK LIST

#	Item	Status	Done (X)
1	**Hospital Bed**		
2	**Bedside Commode**		
3	**Pillows**		
4	**Neck Rest**		
5	**Afghan or Cover up**		
6	**Sheets and mattress Pads** Note: You will need twin-extra long sheets and mattress pads.		
7	**Foot Rest**		
8	**Cane**		
9	**Walker**		
10	**Wheelchair**		
11	**Bedside Table**		
12	**TV Trays**		
13	**Green Plant**		
14	**Containers for Supplies**		
15	**Urinals**		
16	**Trash Cans**		
17	**Bottled Water**		
18	**Plastic Bags for TV Trays or Bedside Tray**		
19	**Plastic Runners**		
20	**Carpet Runners**		
21	**Book shelves or Nite Stand for Storage**		
22	**List of Medications with RX# & Medical Record #**		

SICKROOM CHECK LIST
(Continued)

#	Item	Status	Done (X)
23	**Daily Pill Set Up Container(s)**		
24	**Key Contact Numbers**		
25	**Underwear & Socks**		
26	**House slippers**		
27	**PJ's/Gowns**		
28	**Bathing Supplies**		
29	**Room Deodorizer**		
30	**Books**		
31	**Reading Light**		
32	**Calendar**		
33	**Pens, Pencils & Holder**		
34	**Scratch Pads**		
35	**Container for Snacks**		
36	**Post A Notes**		
37	**Telephone**		
38	**Cell phone**		
39	**Telephone Book**		
40	**Green Plants**		
41	**Television**		
42	**CD Player or Tape Deck**		
43	**Remote Controls Holder**		
44	**Side Chairs for Guests**		
45	**TV Guide**		
46	**Intercom or Bell**		
47	**Travel Mugs**		
48	**Extension Cords**		

#	Item	Status	Done (X)
50	**Large Bath Towels for Spillage**		
51	**Roll of Paper Towels**		
52	**Kleenex**		
53	**Clorox Wipes**		
54	**Straws**		
55	**Pictures of Family**		
56	**Basket for Greeting Cards**		
57	**Identified Location for Medical Record Binder (Hospice)**		
58	**Small Fan to Freshen Up Room**		
59			
60			
61			
62			
63			
64			
65			
66			
67			
68			
69			
70			
71			
72			
73			
74			
75			
76			

#	Item	Status	Done (X)
77			
78			
79			
80			
81			
82			
83			
84			
85			
86			
87			
88			
89			
90			
99			
91			
92			
93			
94			
95			
96			
97			
98			
99			
100			

HOMECARE
ACTION ITEMS

Action Item	Description	Comments

Name: _____
Medical Record Number: _____

LIST OF MEDICATIONS

Medication Prescription/ Non-Prescription	RX#	Unit	Dosage	Frequency	Comments

Name: _____

DAILY DIARY

Date: _____

Caregiver: _____

Woke Up: _____
Urine Output:
Blood Sugar Reading:
____**Units of "N"**
____**Units of "N"**
____**AM Meds**
____**PM Meds**
Bath ___**Yes** ____**No**
BM ____**Yes** ____**No**

Vital Signs
Blood Pressure:
_____
Temperature:
_____
Pulse:
_____

Meals

Breakfast	Lunch	Dinner	Snacks

Activity Level:

_____
_____
_____
_____

Comments:

_____
_____
_____
_____
_____

Questions:

_____
_____
_____
_____
_____
_____
_____
_____
_____

HEALTHCARE
CONTACTS

Name	Relationship to Patient	Phone Numbers Home, Work, Cell	Comments

Name: _____

Medical Record Number: _____

RESPITE CALENDAR

Date	AM	AM	PM	PM	Comments

Name: _____ Name: _____

Phone: _____ Phone: _____

Name: _____ Name: _____

Phone: _____ Phone: _____

Legal Matters

Dotting the i's and Crossing the t's

Land mine (noun), What is a land mine? : 1 : a mine usually placed on or just below the surface of the ground and designed to be exploded usually by the weight of vehicles or troops passing over it; 2 : BOOBY TRAP.

Merriam Webster

For some reason, people have an almost child-like approach to handling death-related matters such as estate planning. Many figure that if they don't discuss it, then it won't happen. Well, I have a news flash for you— plan it or don't plan, it will happen! Just because you do some estate planning, this act will not suddenly hasten your death.

Unfortunately, both marriage and death can bring out the best and the WORST in people— yes, even people in your family. I am surprised when I hear today that there are some spouses who are totally clueless about where the insurance policies or key financial papers are located or even where the checkbook is kept. I guess it still happens, but it is still a surprise to me. If this is your situation, you may have to push this issue with your loved one. If there are changes that need to be made, you both can do it in a timely manner and at a less stressful time.

When Rick was filling out some necessary paperwork prior to his death, the Air Force representative told us that I was not listed as his spouse on his disability paperwork. Rick was rated as disabled by the Air Force prior to our marriage, but had not made that change to his official military paperwork after our marriage. Had that change been made earlier, he would have had additional income during our marriage. We made the change immediately and it was one less issue to take care of later. This is only a small example of what can occur. Whether you are dealing with surgery, catastrophic illness or impending death, I urge you to go over all transactional items with a fine-tooth comb to ensure that the information is current.

Estate Planning

There are a lot of horror stories are circulating regarding people who did not have proper estate planning. As a result, millions of dollars were needlessly paid to Uncle Sam in inheritance taxes and etc. You don't have to be a B-zillionaire to do estate planning. Proper estate planning is particularly important if you have a **blended family** or you came into the marriage with separate assets. Iron out these details well in advance so that there are no "Who-shot-John issues" when one of you has died. The amount you pay for these legal documents will depend upon whether you want a will or full estate planning. Yes, you will most likely have to pay someone to do this, usually an attorney. I suggest that you check the Internet for more detailed information. Heck, everything is on the Internet. By doing some research on the Internet, you will be able ask more intelligent questions and be armed with key information when you actually sit down with an estate planner. Obtaining information on a previously unknown subject is a confidence builder. From a practical point of view, you will usually minimize your consultation fees with the planner if you go into this meeting with an idea of what you think you want. Your estate planner will then be able to tell you the pros and cons of each option, based upon your unique situation.

Another option for you is to go to your local Staples or Office Max store and look at their business forms. Adams Business Forms is an option. When I was at Staples, I noticed that they had packages on Estate Planning, Wills and Durable Power of Attorney. These packages contain valuable information and will walk you through all aspects of the process. You can follow those directions and you create your own documentation. The other option is buy the package, familiarize yourself with the documents and be better informed when you actually meet with your legal consultant.

Rick and I didn't have too many hiccups regarding our estate or financial obligations. However, don't be surprised, if you receive some unsubstantiated claims from ghosts of the past or others who are opportunists. These people slither out from under a rock and sadly want to pick the flesh of the dying. Death will bring out the best and the worst in many people. Be forever vigilant.

A month or two after his death, I became extremely preoccupied with preparing my own estate planning and crossing my t's and dotting my i's. Anyone who knows me knows that I am a contortionist when it comes to detail and being *fair*. The variety of issues that bubble just under the surface and that can crop up may stop you dead in your tracks (pardon the pun). It was during this full disclosure of being fair that I found myself going from keeping people in my estate planning loop to then ALLOWING MYSELF to be backed into a corner justifying what I was planning to do with MY ESTATE. Did I say that it was MY ESTATE? Gather whatever baseline information you may need, make your decisions, ***and then keep your trap shut***. You will be in a state of emotional flux and this will only add angst to an already volatile situation. Develop your master plan for your estate and ensure that it is carried out by someone you trust. This can be done by a trusted friend, a rational family member or a paid trustee. Think before you opt to discuss any of the intimate financial details with your family members or friends. This might open up issues you don't want to discuss at this time. Your family and friends will find out your wishes soon enough after you have slipped over to the other side. *Sheesssssssssssh!!!*

Please note this DISCLAIMER: I am not pretending to be an attorney or an estate planner, but am strongly suggesting that you need to get something in writing. If you don't formally lay out your estate plans, it could cost you in so many ways. We had a family member who died, but had not changed his beneficiary on his insurance policy. He had left his life insurance to his son and had not changed the beneficiary forms to include his new wife.

Well, the son died and then he died, and the wife was not able to claim the insurance. All of this could have been avoided with just a bit of estate planning and proper record keeping.

Review All Contracts and Legal Documents

Before things get really crazy, review all contracts and legal documents for any errors or omissions. This should be done in on a regular basis, regardless of whether you are dealing with an illness or death. Here are just a few thoughts on this subject:

☐ Look at any credit cards to see if you opted for death insurance, etc. If so, this would allow you make an easier financial transition upon the death of your loved one.

☐ Establish a credit line in your own name, if you haven't already done so.

☐ If you have multiple credit union or bank accounts, consider consolidating them. This will allow you to leverage your position with that financial institution, as well as simplifying the management of your finances.

☐ Review the registration of your vehicles. When Rick purchased his truck, I was not with him. He put the registration in his name only. If we had not changed this prior to his death, I would have had a harder time selling the truck.

☐ Car insurance. I continued to pay the insurance premiums for dual drivers on both of our vehicles, when Rick was unable to drive for almost a year before he died. Since I was younger and had a stronger driving record, I could have had a lower premium and saved a nice chunk of money if I was listed as the sole driver. In a distracted state, I didn't even think about this variable. However, up until the last couple of months before his death, Rick was convinced that he would be driving his truck again. It wasn't until one night when he got up by himself, fell, cut his head open and I had to pick him literally up off the floor did he realize that he was no longer strong enough to ever drive his truck again.

☐ Make sure, if there is a safety deposit box that everyone who is supposed to have access to the box signs the signature card for valid entry. If the only valid signer dies, no one else can get into the safety deposit box without the assistance of an attorney, even if the box is attached to an account held in joint tenancy.

Durable Powers of Attorney

In the event that your loved one or you become incapacitated, it is imperative that you have a Durable Power of Attorney for Health Care and a Power of Attorney for your Financial Affairs. Most major medical systems make advance directive available at no charge. These are legal with either two witnesses or a notary stamp. Both are not needed. Please note that an assigned agent, one who will receive benefits from the distribution of the assets, cannot be a valid witness. With the Privacy Laws and the Health Insurance Portability and Accountability Act (HIPPA), you might be stonewalled if this information is not on file or in your possession. Make an appointment with your attorney or research this matter on the Internet to find out what you need to do. There are blank forms that you can download from the Internet to create your own document following their specific directions. There may be a charge, but in view of the importance of these documents, this is imperative.

Once you have a valid document, take it to your health management organization and they will scan it into their system and it will be on file for any future reference. Keep a copy with you in your accordion file in the event that you are asked for it.

Budget

You need to have a clear idea of what your current expenses and income are today and what they will be if one of you dies. I teach a budgeting seminar entitled, "Budgeting for the Not So Rich and Famous." One thing that I stress is that a **budget is not a list of bills.** You need to dissect every aspect of your spending habits to clearly understand your monthly expenses. I would suggest keeping a monthly log of every amount that you spend. While this might be a bit taxing at first, this exercise will allow you to find out where the "leakage" is in your personal finances. It will be a real eye-opener. There should be no normal household expense that comes up that is a surprise. If you pay your car license every year, for example, this amount should be divided by 12 and then placed in a separate household bank account which is not part of your long term savings account. When the registration tags are due, you don't have to scramble nor do a back flip looking for the money. This is true of everything that you purchase. If you buy your kids shoes about every three months and it costs $50.00 a pair that equals about $200.00 a year. Then about $17.00 a month, per child, needs to be placed in this household account. Try keeping a financial log for a couple of months of all of your expenses. Rick and I even got it down to a point that we used an accordion file to drop in the money for the cleaners, food, and movies, etc. It let us properly budget and we avoided many unnecessary trips to the ATM.

This budgeting process is even more crucial if you are about to lose one of your incomes. Take a good look at your expenses. You may want to make some change. These changes may positively impact your budget. For example, I knew that I would only have one cell phone bill. Review the need for any gym memberships, association dues, the number of times you receive the newspaper or the number of premium cable TV channels in your package (we had them ALL!). Food, gas, and electricity will all be less when there is only one of you at home. This is not being ghoulish, it is being practical, and you will have to figure it out later anyway. Depending on your individual circumstances, you may have to return to work on a full or part-time basis. Finding out what your monthly income and expenses are coupled with developing alternatives is a great stress reliever. Remember: Failing to Plan is Planning to Fail.

Medical Benefits

Make sure that you clearly understand your medical benefits. Even if you think you do, refresh your level of understanding by first rereading your documentation and then talking to the medical provider's representative or personnel office. Your employee and/or retirement benefits may have changed since you initially started working for your company or retired. Whenever you are talking to anyone on these matters and you have to contact them again, find out if there is a direct dial number that you can call to save time. Also make sure that you jot down the first and last name of the representative that you are speaking to and the date that you made the call. Again, log this information in your handy-dandy spiral notebook.

☐ **Long-Term Healthcare Insurance**: This is an excellent program and one that assisted Rick and me tremendously. This program will allow you to have additional medical assistance in the event that you have a long term illness or need help in your own home or in a nursing home. You will not have to burn through your savings in order to properly take care of your loved one before Medicare kicks in. Having long-term healthcare insurance can be the difference between keeping your home or possibly losing it. The premiums are determined by your age. There also may be a provision for you to lock in your rate at a slightly higher amount and no be impacted by premium increases. Again, check at your job and with your insurance carrier to find out the details specific to your plan, regarding fulfilling any *waiting period* before your full benefits start.

☐ **Military Benefits**: Those who were in the armed services of our country may be eligible for military benefits to assist with an illness. You can call or go to the local base and ask to speak to a Veterans Service Officer or similar representative to determine if you have an issue that is eligible for coverage as a veteran. Your loved one and or their dependents might also be eligible for veterans' funeral and burial benefits. An excellent web site for frequently asked questions is: http://www.funerals.or/faq/vet.htm. *Again, do a bit of research on the Internet and then you will be able to ask informed questions when you call your Veterans Administration Representative.* I have worked with these representatives and they were absolutely wonderful and will bend over backwards to help a veteran or his/her family.

☐ Make a list of companies that you will have to contact in order to inform them of the death of your loved one and to make a name change, if your loved one dies. Doing this will not make them die any sooner, but will allow you or your representative to make these changes in an orderly manner during an extremely trying time in your lives.

Social Security, Pensions, Etc.

This is a complicated area, but I will give you a couple of places to start:

Social Security Benefits

To take it or not to take it is the question. Depending on your age, there is a sliding scale on the amount of benefits that you receive. I would be nuts to try to explain all of this to you. I do know that if I were younger than 60 years of

age, I would not have been eligible to receive Rick's social security survivors' benefit. However, you should contact the Social Security Administration on this matter. I called a representative in advance of Rick's death (surprised?) after I had downloaded a bunch of information to make sure that I was properly informed. I have found their representatives tremendously helpful. Their website, www.socialsecurity.gov, is easy to navigate and there is a section on Frequently Asked Questions. The toll-free number to reach a representative is 1-800-772-1213. Even if you are widowed and take your reduced spousal benefit, you will be able to then file your own claim when you are 62+. Social Security will give you the higher of the two benefits. You don't get both your benefit and his/her benefit. Please take the time to review this information as it will arm you with information that will allow you to move more easily through this process.

I found out a lot about the processing of a social security claim when I helped a neighbor with the final arrangements and business issues after the death of her husband. While I received my first benefit check within a month, it may take up to two months for a spouse or eligible family member to actually receive Survivor's Benefits based on other variables. This may not seem like a big deal if you don't depend on the social security check. However, for many people this is not the case. *It is imperative that you have at least two times the anticipated monthly social security check amount in a separate account to cover this potential waiting period.* This fund will minimize your financial difficulties while the Social Security Payment Center is processing your claim. Also I found out that the payments are made in arrears and reflect the earned benefit for the previous month. The initial payment also reflected a one-time payment of $255.00 for "flowers." I can only assume that this amount was more practical years ago when there was less paperwork. In today's bureaucracy by the time you receive this money a month or two later, you have probably already spent money on flowers.

For easy reference make sure that you get the name and the date of your contact with Social Security. Record this information in your spiral notebook.

Family Medical Leave Act (FMLA)

I was fortunate enough to be retired when Rick was sick and did not have the pressures of taking care of a dying spouse and holding down a job. This may not be the case for you. Check with your personnel office to find out if you are eligible for FMLA. FMLA allows you to take extra time off beyond the time that you have accrued on the books to deal with a family illness.

A Synopsis of Law U.S. Department of Labor states:

> "Covered employers must grant an eligible employee up to a total of 12 work weeks of unpaid leave during any 12-month period for one or more of the following reasons:
>
> - for the birth and care of the newborn child of the employee;
> - for placement with the employee of a son or daughter for adoption or foster care;
> - to care for an immediate family member (spouse, child, or parent) with a serious health condition; **or**
> - to take medical leave when the employee is unable to work because of a serious health condition ...."

For additional information, please go to the Department of Labor website, http://www.dol.gov/esa/whd/fmla/. You will find a series of Frequently Asked Questions which will answer a majority of your questions.

This formal process will ensure that you still have a job if you have to use a lot of sick leave. You will need to have sufficient sick leave or vacation hours to cover any time taken to handle family medical issues. Now, you are expected to pull your own weight when you are at work, but you will be given a certain amount of leeway due to increased absences because of personal or family illness. Your co-workers can help, too. When I worked for the State of California, if an employee needed to use FMLA for a catastrophic illness— either their illness or that of a family member— and did not have enough personal, sick or vacation days to do so, the required time could be donated by other employees. This was an optional process. There is a specific process to become eligible for FMLA. Check with your personnel office to see about this concept and whether or not your situation qualifies for FMLA.

Listing of Key Legal Contacts

During this entire process, you will be collecting important phone numbers and contacts. I would suggest that you write them down for easy reference. If you are comfortable with the computer, you should use it and then date each version of the document to ensure that you are referencing the latest information. Microsoft Excel or Word are efficient tools to use to capture this information.

Here is a sample matrix of the key contacts that I have made during my process:

FINANCIAL MATTERS
KEY CONTACTS

Category	Timeline	Contact Phone Number	Required Documents	Status	Comments
Investments	ASAP		Death Certificate	Call Financial Planner's Office	
Retirement or Pensions	ASAP		Death Certificate		
Insurance Policies			Death Certificate	Find out what the procedure is way in advance	
Your Banks and Credit Unions				You might want to simplify this if you both have separate accounts.	
Social Security Administration		1-800-772-1213	Death Certificate	The funeral director may also make the call to Social Security Office and notify them of the death. There is a one time benefit of $255 for flowers. Call the 1-800 # to get an appointment locally.	
Health Club Membership					
Newspaper				You might want to take the paper for fewer week days.	
Magazine Subscriptions				Some of these may be eliminated.	
Credit Unions					
Cable TV				We no longer needed all of the premium channels because I was not a big television watcher.	

Pre-Need Funeral Planning

There is a phenomenal website, http//www.funeralwithlove.com/funeral.htm that is a storehouse of valuable information. This site even has a Funeral Calculator so that you can get a good estimate of potential funeral expenses. It also discusses the different types of services and many other subjects. Visit this site or your local bookstore for related information. Here is a sample of my form:

FUNERAL PLANNING
KEY CONTACTS

Category	Timeline	Contact Phone Number	Required Documents	Status	Comments
Obituary				WRITE IT NOW. Don't leave something this important up to chance. Do your kids really know where you went to school or what your aspirations are?	
Assistance With Funeral Arrangements		1-800-531-5803 (916) 452-4444	DD214 (Separation Document)	Contact Air Force Mortuary department for specifics or the funeral director will handle this matter. Work with Morgan and Jones Funeral Home for directions.	
Federal Assistance With Funeral Arrangements		1-877-645-466	DD214 (Separation Document)	Honors Unit. Contact these people to secure an Honor Guard for full military service. When asked for a code, use Code 33634 Contact these people for specifics or the funeral director will handle this matter.	
Obituary in Sacramento Bee		(916) 321-1000		Bea has written and needs to do the final work on this. Find out the costs	
Memory Cards with Photo				Contact Deanna to find out where she got the memory cards that she handed out for Freddie. Use the formal picture of Rick smiling. It is in the frame on the counter in the upstairs hallway.	
Memorial or Funeral Program				Start this way in advance. Make sure that you contact the people who you want to participate in the service way ahead of time.	

The important fact is that you start this list now. Based upon what you find out, you will then know the **NUMBER OF DEATH CERTIFICATES** that you will ultimately need. In the event that you need a certified copy of the Birth Certificate, you will have known this in advance and will have had enough time to find it or order a replacement. There will be a lot of fumbling and stumbling while you are preparing for the services, etc. You will be way ahead of the process if you have this information at your fingertips. This subject is discussed in more detail in the chapter entitled, "Traditional Funeral Plans."

NOTE: I ordered 10 death certificates and found out that I really didn't need that many. Most organizations wanted to make a COPY of a certified Death Certificate and few actually wanted an original copy. But, I have them and won't have to go through a bunch of hoops ordering more if I need them in the future.

If at all possible, assist your loved one in writing his or her obituary. This will ensure that you have the information correct and complete. Even if you do this, there may be family members or friends who get bent out of shape because something wasn't included in the printed obituary. You can't anticipate or worry about this issue.

And, by the way, have you written YOUR obituary? Oh, you don't have one? Then start one right away! To help you in this regard, I have created an **Obituary Worksheet**. Please use this document to jot down key facts regarding your life. This can be basis for you to write your own obituary in advance or for your loved ones so do after you have passed on. This will eliminate the scurrying around that occurs when they will have to try to put together your obituary without all of the pertinent facts. I suggest that you draft out your obituary and e-mail it to a key person or at least include it in a Funeral or Celebration of Life folder that you can label and put in your file cabinet or safety deposit box.

LEGAL MATTERS
ACTION ITEMS

Done (X)	Item	Required Action	Status	Comments

Obituary Worksheet

Done (X)	Obituary Element	Facts
	Full Name	
	Date of Birth	
	Date of Death	
	Parents Name	
	Location of Birth	
	Step-Parents' Names	
	Names of Siblings and their Spouses	
	Places Lived	
	Schools Attended	
	Degrees Obtained	
	Significant Life Events as a child	
	Significant Life Events as teen	
	Significant Life Events as an Adult	
	First Marriage and events	
	Second Marriage and events	
	Children	

Obituary Worksheet
(Continued)

Done (X)	Obituary Element	Facts
	Grandchildren	
	Other Relatives	
	Work Experience	
	Hobbies	
	Places Traveled	
	Best Friends	
	Special Events	
	Church Affiliation(s)	
	Professional Associations	
	Favorite Poem or Saying	
	Funeral or Memorial Information	
	Burial Information	
	Contributions in lieu of flowers	
	Military Affiliation	
	Pets	

Keeping your Sanity

"Help me. I'm melting, I'm melting..."
—The Wicked Witch from the Wizard of Oz

*"When you come to the end of all the light you know, and it's time
to step into the darkness of the unknown, faith is knowing that
one of two things will happen: Either you will be given
something solid to stand on or you will be taught to fly."*

—Edward Teller

Some illnesses may go on for a few months or several years. This entire process exacts a toll on the caregiver. "They" say that the caregiver is the "first to go". Unless you have been a caregiver, you won't really understand this comment. While taking care of Rick, I was admitted to the hospital twice. Once the doctors thought I was having a heart attack and the other time I showed all the symptoms of having a blood clot in my lungs! Bottom line, it was stress … mountains and mountains of stress.

During one of these emergency room visits, I was talking on the phone with Joan A, who was lambasting me for driving myself to the ER. As we were talking, the most gorgeous Black doctor walked into the room. I, being a fan of the television show, *Grey's Anatomy*, mumbled into the phone that I had to go because although "Dr. McDreamy" wasn't on call tonight, a "Dr. McChocolate" just came into my room and I wanted to give him all of my attention. Ladies; he was definitely worth the trip to the ER! Whewwww!

Keeping your sanity is the hardest thing that you will attempt to do at this time. If you are out of your mind, like I was, maybe it is because you are trying to do everything yourself. You can't do everything yourself and maintain your sanity. It is physically impossible to carry your weight and the weight of another person and not bend under this obligation.

To vent your frustrations is not being a cry baby. I had one distant "friend" tell me that I need not be concerned about my feelings, that all that really mattered was how I took care of Rick. ***This is a crock and I want to be the first to tell you this.*** You HAVE to also be aware of how you are feeling and make sure that you are taking care of both your body and your soul/spirit. Being a caregiver is NOT for the faint of heart and you will find out that you are far more human than you thought. By the way, this "friend" later had all types of serious health issues that had started when she became a dual caregiver and simply ignored her physical and spiritual needs. *It is not necessary for you to fall into this martyred category.* It is a highly overrated category!

A well-meaning person may say to you that you are "too blessed to be stressed!" This is a nice little conceptual religious phrase, but blessed or not, this entire process will leave you stressed. Hint: YOU ARE HUMAN and will find that if you are cut, you will definitely bleed. But, don't lash out at these people. From time to time you will want to lash out, but it is a lot like the naked man who jumped on the cactus bush … it seemed like a good idea at the time.

However, I thought that I would share some situations I encountered so that you can be *forewarned* and, therefore, *forearmed*.

Naysayers

When the Naysayers show themselves, kindly smile, go the other way and keep any future plans to yourself. I wasn't prepared for these types of negative interactions. These people can bring you down and make you doubt yourself. Avoid them. Some topics are meant for general discussion, others are not. You will find out what you can say and to whom you can say it. It is a trial-and-error process. I learned to emulate a matador during most of this process. When a matador **sees the "bull"** coming their way, they just step to the side without any grand motion or anger and say, *olé* and let the "beast" pass right on by. Some days I won, and some days I got severely gored.

When I mentioned to some of my *"understanding"* friends that I was taking a brief respite from my caregiver duties, I was surprised that some of them expressed shock. Once they found out that I was taking a trip by myself and *leaving* Rick at home I got about 18 yards of guilt laid on me for "leaving" my poor sick husband. *Well this just blew my hair back!* When I shared my concern about these comments to Rick, he firmly stated that there were only TWO people whose opinions mattered in this situation—his and mine—period. These people meant no harm, but clearly had not walked an inch in my shoes let alone a mile in my shoes. Little did they know but I was quietly heading for a nervous breakdown.

Take your respite breaks. You are not being selfish because have decided to take care of yourself. In taking a break, you can take better care of your loved one and ultimately yourself. In fact, both our long term health insurance representatives and hospice personnel encouraged me to take respite breaks. These respite breaks are built into both programs because the stressors on the caregiver are recognized by these organizations and these breaks are a known necessity for the caregiver.

The following elements were essential to helping me find balance during this trying period. Some of these suggestions may very well lessen your stress.

Faith

OK, I am a practicing Christian and was raised in the church. You will see a sprinkling of Christianity throughout this book because it is an integral part of the fabric of Bea Bailey. I came to really know the Lord on my own as an adult and not as part of a family tradition as child. My faith and belief have helped me and opened emotional doors that I didn't even know were there. My St. Paul Family, particularly my Small Accountability Group (SAG) #11, were there to support me when I couldn't even put two words or steps together. I began to read the Bible with a new level of awareness and understanding. The words were no longer something written a long time ago by some old people in really funny clothes. They were now an integral part of my life.

When I would pray, sometimes I would be so overwhelmed that I would just be there on my knees babbling or making another list of things to do in my head. I know that God knew my heart and continued to bless me in the midst of my personal storms. Christianity works for me. The purpose of this book is not to convert you to Christianity… that might be another book. Whatever your personal faith or belief system is, tap into it to sustain you and brush away the many emotional cobwebs that you will find crossing your path.

Even WITH my faith, there were days that I wanted to run from the house screaming. On my many walks I had to wonder out loud how I would be coping WITHOUT my faith.

Scream Buddy

What the devil is a Scream Buddy?

Moses had Aaron, Oprah has Gail, Bonnie had Clyde and you have _____? This is a person to whom you can go and, literally or figuratively, scream your fool head off, kick, cry, or yell. Your Scream Buddy will not pass judgment. He or she will let you vent and then offer you a tissue, a stiff drink, some chocolate or keep sharp objects out of your way. Once you have finished, he or she will often ask you what you now plan to do about this issue or simply ask you to pass the potatoes and say nothing. They may have an answer—or maybe just tell you that you need to come back next week for another scream session.

I am fortunate enough to have two—Ruth (Rayuth) and Rosemary (R^2). I have known Ruth for 35+ years and Rosemary for 25+ years. We are as different visually as two friends can be, yet have so much in common. I am almost 6 feet tall and Black. Ruth is a towering 5'5"and R^2 is 5'2". Both of these ladies are translucent in color but are individual forces of nature. In the time of trouble, you want one of them on your team at all times. I was blessed to have both of them on my team.

Ruth and I have raised our children together, and she helped me with my struggles to get out of my first marriage, with the bumps and bruises of single life, and to deal with the ups and downs of my second marriage.

She knows me so well and has not (huh, Ruth?) passed judgment on me when we would laugh and cry together. We are truly sisters, but just don't have the same mother or father. She sat and cried with me as I picked out Rick's coffin and walked beside me when I went to bury him. Ruth and I even found things about which to laugh. Why on-earth would you need a coffin with a drawer that had a LOCK AND KEY? Was the man going to get up in the middle of the night and look for his cuff links? We both burst out laughing. Ruth has always proven to be my touchstone in life. I will be eternally grateful to her for steering me from the many edges of insanity that I have teetered on throughout my life and sometimes just telling me to shut-up and listen.

Rosemary (R^2) and I became friends when she was my manager at Xerox. I was pretty independent and successful, I might add, as a Marketing Representative. When I was promoted to Account Representative, I decided that the last thing I needed was a new little five-foot manager, from Texas of all places, rocking my world and telling me what to do. I set up a meeting so that I could put her in her place. I met with her and told her that I was independent and that I needed little management. If there was a problem, I would let her know. Rosemary told me that that was nice, but until I earned the right to run my territory independently, I would be treated like every other sales representative that she managed. OK apparently, there was a new sheriff in town and she was going to kick some serious butt... mine included. During our early years, if she told me as my sales manager to jump off a building, I would do so, no questions asked. However, after a year of this, I still would jump off the building, but would ask a couple of second level questions before I jumped. Rosemary is a no-holds-barred tough lady that has been an anchor in my life. With one or two words, she can freeze water at 30 paces or melt you into a puddle of warm chocolate.

While not exactly Scream Buddies, my sisters—Ellouise, Diane and Deborah—and brother, Wendell, were also a tremendous support system. They would check on me, chastise me, if necessary, but were always there to help me. It was as if the entire "sister dynamics" (and you know what I am talking about), were gone. They were there to help me whenever I would begin to stumble or fall or bump into one wall after another. I was always the one that the family called "Little Miss Independent" and always had *IT* together. Well, if I did, I certainly couldn't find it during the final phase of Rick's illness. It sounds soooooooo corny, but they have proven to truly be the wind beneath my wings when I was unable to fly by myself.

My sister Debbie is the youngest and has a well-earned reputation of being a force of nature. I, on the other hand, have always been the "older", dutiful sister. However, during the course of Rick's illness, it was total role reversal and she treated me with such loving kindness and support that it astounded me and often brought me to tears. And, then there is my brother Wendell… he was always the steady Eddy and a beacon of unconditional love and support for me.

My sister, Ellouise was also a tremendous support. Of course, if she said, _"Today is today and tomorrow is tomorrow. Just take it one day at a time"_ one more time, I was going to fly back to Iowa and knock her out. She has been a constant throughout this entire process and has provided me with unwavering support and tenderness. She has walked a bit in my shoes, having a husband with a myriad of health issues.

My sister, Diane, was a gem. She always seemed to send me the appropriate card when I was dragging around the house. Diane also wrote a federal grant at her school on how children handled death and dying. I have listed many of the books that she suggested in the Reference Section of this book.

I also received a lot of support from my artsy-creative friend Mona, founder of the Monart Art Institute, www.monart.com. We have known each other for years when we worked together for the State of California. I used to call her and disguise my voice on many occasions. She just loved Rick to death (pardon the pun) and when he took a turn for the worse, she came up immediately to see about him. In the door she came, put her stuff in "her" room, took off her shoes and climbed in the hospital bed with Rick. They were big movie buffs and they would just lay there quietly watching TV while I prepared dinner. The next night, all three of us piled into the hide-a-bed in the office upstairs to watch television. We had snacks and watched a couple of movies. It was like a big, old slumber party and Rick really enjoyed himself. Not a lot was said. If you are close to someone, not a lot needs to be said. Actions speak louder than words.

Last, but not least, is my neighbor, Cindy F., "Mi` Hermanita." She is one of the most interesting and funny people I have EVER met. She is a tea master (Tea Anytime), an antique dealer, expert shopper, interior designer, master gardener, world traveler and precious stones expert. She has lived life to its fullest and would always make herself available to me in so many ways. Cindy always told me that I was doing a good job taking care of "Richard", but I needed to make sure that I was taking care of myself. She even tried to get me to start planning my life when Rick was gone. We would discuss from time to time how I needed to eventually redecorate the house. Cindy always spoke to me about retooling my future as a way of distracting me from the daily responsibilities of taking care of a dying husband. She has the unique ability to pop over for a visit when I was feeling sad and say something off the wall to cheer me up.

The key is that your Scream Buddies do not pass judgment. If they do, they keep it to themselves. They are unconditional vessels that will allow you to vent in a safety zone. ***Someone who has been a caregiver is an excellent choice*** when you are looking for a scream buddy. Unless you have walked in the shoes of a caregiver, you have no clue as to what I am even trying to say here. Mary C. (Mary's Alternations) was a former caregiver. She told me that I will get insensitive comments from family or friends regarding any level of frustration I had in being a caregiver. However, I have to remember that they love Rick but, as his caregiver I love him as well, but have the weight of taking care of him everyday.

Sometimes these Scream Buddy sessions are quite fruitful, and you will come away with a lot of solutions and insights into what is going on inside of you. I have found that when I would leave one of these sessions, I felt calmer and more centered. Sometimes you may leave in the same emotional state. It is not an exact science.

Pamper Yourself

There are a variety of strategies you may want to consider when you are under stress. One strategy is pampering yourself. Here are some pampering suggestions:

☐ **Housekeeper**

For goodness sake, get a housekeeper if you can! Or press into service the many friends who say that they want to help, but just need a bit of direction. If not, make a deal with yourself to just keep the company areas neat and worry about the rest of the house later. I had the downstairs of our house set up as Rick's sick room and had everything pretty wired and organized. Anyone who knows me knows that I am a pretty neat person. However, if anyone came upstairs and looked at my bedroom or the rest of the rooms upstairs, they would have thought that I had just moved into the house. Sometimes, I would just come upstairs, drop stuff or step over stuff and flop on the bed. There were good days and bad days. Some organized days and some really disorganized days.

☐ **Beauty or Barber Shop Appointments**

I normally went about every couple of weeks to the beauty shop. The atmosphere at Inner Beauty is very holistic and healing. It was like going to a group therapy session each time that I went. Once, I was so nervous and upset when I went for a hair appointment with Carla, my beautician, that I started watering her plants to calm my nerves. Well, the plants were pretty dry and the water just ran right out the bottom of the pots. I flooded the counters and part of the floor. One of her employees, yelled, "Oh Lord, it is Hurricane Katrina!" Carla calmly sat me down and began to rub lavender oil on my temples to calm me before she could even start doing my hair.

☐ **Massage Therapy**

During this caretaker phase of your life, you are giving, giving and then doing more giving. One healing element is the human touch. If you can afford it, treat yourself to a massage from time to time. Just a half hour of focused massage can do wonders for you both physically and mentally. Even a hand-held massager on the base of your neck, forehead and temples can be a great tension reliever. Check with your local herbalist for some lavender essential oil. I would sprinkle some of this on my pillow at night to help me sleep.

☐ **Chiropractic Therapy**.

We were blessed have a skilled chiropractor, John Johnsrud (Dr. "J"), www.johnsrudchiropractic.com. He monitored both Rick's health and my resulting stress. "Dr. J" informed me that when you are under stress your body is in a "demand" state. This is a chiropractic term indicating the effect of stress on your body. As a result, I would have periodic chiropractic adjustment with Dr. "J" to deal with the stress that I seemed to carry in my neck and lower back.

☐ **Exercise Routine and/or Personal Trainer**

While I am admittedly a bit of a gym rat, I would strongly recommend some type of physical exercise program. If you belong to a gym, use that gym…"duh." If not, then join one. If you are not the "gym" type, then start walking and increase your distances. Take some sort of class, such as exercise, dance; yoga or tap that will tax your body a bit. When you work out —your body releases happy enzymes called endorphins. They are the body's natural opium that increases the feeling of well-being. When I walk in my neighborhood, the course is exactly 1.3 miles. I normally walk around twice. I use the first leg to thank God for all that he had done for me and my family and the ability to be able to take this walk unaided. During the second time around, I normally beg for stuff. You can use that time to meditate or do a silent scream or whatever—*but get off that couch and move and release those happy endorphins.* Whatever you decide to do, consistency is the key.

Jake T., my **24-Hour Fitness** personal trainer and **certified Russian kettlebell instructor,** also kept me sane during Rick's illness and death. As we worked out with the **kettlebells,** he always told me to "*tighten my abs, keep my back straight and my butt down!*" However during these weekly workouts, Jake also dealt with both my physical training and emotional needs. I will be eternally grateful to Jake for constantly propping me up on the many occasions when I was emotionally falling apart.

The common thread in all of these suggestions is that you will have an hour or so where the *only thing you have to do is let someone else take care of you.* By doing this, you will find yourself more refreshed and able to run your personal race with more vigor and stamina.

Professional Support

The Watermelon Story

I would like to share a story with you on being under tremendous stress and not even knowing it. It has now become my now infamous "Watermelon Story." After we found out that Rick had stage 4 lung cancer, I tried to find mini day trips to distract him from the deteriorating condition of his health. He was pretty compromised due to the side

effect of his chemotherapy treatments. One field trip was out in the country to Sloughhouse's vegetable stand. It was at the end of watermelon season, but I decided to pick one up for him since he loved them so much. In order to make things convenient for him and give him a sense of independence, I would cut up the watermelon and put it in individual containers. All Rick had to do was open the fridge and help himself.

After doing this, I decided to dish up a large bowl of watermelon for myself and go upstairs and watch TV. When I sat down, I reached for the watermelon and it wasn't there. I waited for the first commercial to go downstairs and retrieve it. When I went downstairs and looked for the watermelon, it wasn't there. Oh well, I thought, I will check upstairs at the next break. Well, I looked for it at the break and couldn't find it. I asked Rick if he had seen it. I then checked the laundry room—nothing there. What the...? I thought. The house is about 2,000 square feet, so it couldn't be in too many places.

Then the phone rang and it was my good buddy, Ruby, calling to check on me. She asked me how I was doing. I told her that I thought that I was losing my mind because I couldn't find the watermelon I had just cut. She asked me if I had retraced my steps and I said that I had. She then asked me if I had eaten it. I said, "heck no," but I wasn't sure. She stayed on the phone with me while I went downstairs. Not only had I EATEN the watermelon, I had put the empty dish in the dishwasher and didn't even remember doing it! Ruby said that she then knew how I was really doing. This was clearly a lot of unrefined free floating stress.

Individual Counseling

Some people have HMO horror stories. I have had the good fortune to have had more positive experiences with Kaiser than negatives ones. During Rick's recovery from his back surgery and the subsequent diagnosis of stage 4 lung cancer, I had a series of office visits to my general practitioner. I went for discoloration on my leg, headaches, a bump on my head, high blood pressure, and the probably galloping gout.

Next, I was admitted into Kaiser's Emergency Room in October 2005 due to severe chest pains and concern over a possible "heart attack." You didn't have to be a brain surgeon to determine that it was stress related. The ER doctor came in and told me that my heart was fine, but he was worried about my spirit. He said that I had to find a way NOT to be at my husband's every beck and call, because it was slowly killing me. I had lost 12 pounds and dropped two pant sizes. I looked like a scarecrow with Shirley Temple curls. What a sight! When you go to the gym and your trainer admonishes you because you are _too thin_...then you are too thin. I knew I had to make some changes in my life to relieve some of the load. What to do, what to do? How do you let go, particularly when you are a control freak? _OK, I admit it._

During my follow-up visit with my personal physician after the ER incident, I was rattling on (as I am sometimes known to do) about what had happened, when she put down her pen, rolled her chair over to me and took me by the hand. She looked me directly in the eye and said, "Bea, what is _really_ bothering you?" Why on earth did she do that? I burst into tears and started sobbing. This is a big thing for me because as Wonder Woman, my tear ducts have been hermetically sealed years ago to prevent the world from knowing that I am human. She said that when someone comes into her office this often, there is something going on in his/her life other than the reason for which the appointment was made. I told her that I couldn't bear seeing Rick die because I felt so helpless. I would rather be somewhere else than to watch his slow physical deterioration. She then recommended that I go and see a counselor, which I did, and it helped a lot.

"I'm as Mad as Hell and I'm Not Going To Take It Anymore!"

Realized and Unrealized Anger

When I married the first time, I would become angry at the kids' father but didn't always show my level of anger. I can remember once walking down the hall near the bedroom and his closet door was open. Instead of addressing my anger to him, I leaned over and bit the sleeve of his shirt that I had just starched and ironed. By cracky, that showed him, I tell you.

You will find yourself being angry from time to time. Sometimes you might KNOW why you are angry as you clean up a pile of diarrhea or a cup of spilled black coffee or chocolate Ensure on your blond living rug. Other times, you might just wake up MAD "cuz" you are bone tired and it looks like the only light at the end of the tunnel is another "dat gum" train. Then you feel guilty and hateful and unworthy and all that self-flagellation begins. This, too, will pass.

Once I remember lamenting my woes to Rosemary and was going on and on in an e-mail to her. We replied back and forth, and she told me that if I planned to do anything foolish, like kill him, I needed to "Wipe down the gun afterwards!" When I read that I couldn't help but burst out laughing and knew that she had been watching way too much "Law and Order" and "CSI". On another occasion, I was belly-aching about something that Rick wasn't doing (before I knew how sick he was) and she simply e-mailed me a three-word response regarding her husband's health: "Mine is blind." That put things into proper prospective and we both had one heck of a belly laugh.

There will also be occasions in which someone's insensitivity will just blow your hair back. Some people will see a widow or a widower as a person with a target on their back. I can remember a specific incident that occurred just after the open house that we had for Rick. I was in the church's parking lot getting ready to attend a Saturday morning meeting. I encountered one of the single gentlemen who had just attended an open house that I had for Rick. He sauntered up to me and extended his arms and said, "Hey, Bea, let me be one of the first ones to get a jump start!" He then came up to me and gave me a great big hug. I was at a loss for words at his level of boldness. *First of all, what was it that he thought needed a jumpstart and why did he think he had what was needed to start IT?* I was so angry that it was a blessing that I was on the church's property or I would have laid him out on the asphalt. Mind you, my husband was still alive at this point. I could only shake my head in total disbelief at this insensitive act.

As a caregiver, you will sleep like a new mother with a newborn in the house, which, of course means that you will not get any sleep. Your ear is always open to any sound regarding your patient. You will be able to attest to your sleep deprivation when you take one of your respite breaks. All night long, I could hear Rick adjusting his bed with the electronic controls. Up, down, and then up, down again. If I heard his footsteps, I would pause and listen for where he was going or even get up and go and see if he needed anything. Once, I was sleeping (or so I thought) and I heard the step on the upstairs landing squeak. It only squeaked when someone stepped on it. I called out, "Rick, is that you?' He said, "Yes." How he made it up the stairs was baffling to me. Rick then crawled into bed with me. Rick said that he just needed to come upstairs and be near me. He then gently took me in his arms and was able to lie with me for about 15 minutes. Next he struggled to get out of bed and made his way back downstairs. He said that he did not want my help getting back downstairs. This was such a poignant and extremely sad moment for me. I lay awake for the rest of the night just thinking about what an act of love he had just demonstrated towards me.

On several occasions, I would go downstairs and sleep in his hospital bed with him. Believe it or not, these two six-foot+ people could actually fit into this tiny space. *Come on, you remember snuggling with your spouse or your significant other is less space that this!* Early on in his sickness I would sleep in his hospital bed with him for an hour or two. However, towards the end, as his body began shutting down, his body was throwing off so much heat that it became uncomfortable for both of us. These occasions of snuggling with him were tender, almost sacred, moments that I will always remember.

The Chicken Coop Story

Everyone says that I look like my grandmother Tishie McKenzie, which I consider a compliment. She is legendary in our family, particularly among the women, for how she dealt with an abusive, belligerent second husband.

One day her husband came home from work and confronted her. My grandmother was quietly sewing when he approached her. He berated her for not cleaning out the chicken coop. Without looking up, she calmly said, "It won't be like that tomorrow." He felt satisfied and went into the other room. Nothing feels better to some men than putting a woman in HER place.

The next day he came home and immediately went out to inspect the chicken coop. Mr. McKenzie found his chickens and the chicken coop burnt to the ground and my grandmother calmly sewing, with a large butcher knife next to her sewing kit. Well, she was a woman of her word. Discretion being the better part of valor, he opted to leave her alone. All the women on my mother's side of the family can stop their husbands in mid-stride, by uttering, "It won't be like that tomorrow." The men immediately say, "Baby, can't we sit down and negotiate a more peaceful solution?"

You must have ways to both vent and then have a really good laugh at yourself and the situation. These feelings are normal and will pass. From time to time, your patient might lash out at you. It is hard _not_ to take this personally when you have been verbally slapped in the face by someone for whom you are doing your best. It isn't even a matter of not being appreciated. I know that you might be angry, but let it go, they really don't mean it. While I know that no one promised me a rose garden but when you get stuck by a thorn, it hurts and you will cry out.

Post-Traumatic Stress Syndrome

Rick had withdrawn a few years prior to his diagnosis of cancer and things had become pretty rocky in our marriage. I was angry at Rick for a long time before he was diagnosed with lung cancer. It seemed that after he retired (18 months earlier) he became even more distant. It was as if all of the wind went out of his sails. He found no joy in anything except the grandchildren's sports events and spent hours in front of the television watching anything about —WWII. We had the History Channel, the Military Channel, and Discovery Channel—any channel that just might have something about the war. If he couldn't find anything on the war, he would put in a video tape he had recorded years ago about the Battle of Midway. He had been in the service for 30 years and it was a great part of who he was. "Hello, Mr. Bailey, I am over here, hello?" Here I was with my nose pressed against the glass screaming, "You are dying and all you want to do is watch movies about the war? *We won, they lost, now get over it!"*

There were way too many silent car rides from one location to another. I was extremely confused because when we use to go anywhere, we always chatted, played word games, and never ran out of things to say to each other. But over the years, this lively banter dissipated and all that was left was the silence… just the oppressive silence.

When our Kaiser Hospice social worker met with us for the first time, she could sense the tension in the home. She asked more in-depth questions and then made her observation. She said that it appeared to her that Rick was suffering from classical Post Traumatic Stress Syndrome (PTSD). He was imbedded deeply in Vietnam and when he returned, he masked his symptoms with heavy drinking. When he stopped drinking, he then continued to watch or read anything about war, particularly, WWII. When he retired and then became sick, he watched TV even more. The social worker said that she would bring me information on PTSD during her next visit and suggested that I check it out on the Internet. I did and found out that it can be triggered by retirement and/or a chronic illness … bingo.

Once I understood the ramifications of this mental illness, I was able to not personalize his withdrawal and better able to understand what was going on inside of him. One form of treatment for PTSD is Prozac coupled with in-depth counseling. Well, he was in the middle of dying and this option made no sense. Had I known more about PTSD, I would have encouraged him earlier in our marriage to seek treatment for this disease. It had gotten to the point that whenever we would sleep together, (when he was not up late watching something about WWII) I had to reposition Rick so that his back was always facing the middle of the bed and his face towards the edge. This was the result of me finding his hands wrapped around my throat on several occasions when he would wake up yelling in the middle of the night with one of his many Viet Nam nightmares. To ease the situation, I used to tell him that this wasn't a marriage it was a nerve wracking adventure! However, there was nothing "funny" about this matter. Rick would have to have acknowledged his behavior as a problem and been the one who sought out this treatment. Rick would then have to follow through the treatment plan to deal with the many nightmares and associated depression that was a result of his two tours of Viet Nam.

The Veterans Administration has established programs to address the effects of PTSD. I encourage all veterans and their families to look into these programs for additional support.

Support Groups

There are many support groups available to help you make the adjustments that you have to make while dealing with the care of a loved one. I had incorrectly thought that all support groups would be like AA, which is wonderful. I had preconceived thoughts that I would come into the room and say, "Hi, my name is Bea. I am a caregiver losing her mind." Then the room would all say, "Hi, Bea!" Well, this is just a misconception I am told. Many people who I have come into contact with have spoken highly of the benefits of belonging to a support group. I did not avail myself of a support group due to the amount of support that I had in so many other areas. I attended one of these sessions after Rick had passed and found that this particular one was not a good fit for me because all they did was talk about the effects of the different kinds of cancers, but definitely served the needs of many people who were in attendance. I was approached by several people in the group who felt that I had a lot of offer them with their situations. I opted out because I just couldn't take on another project. However, I would suggest that you check some out support groups and take them for a test run. Participating in a support group will be a personal decision.

Talk to Other Caregivers

Try and find another person who has been a caregiver. I had negative feelings that I felt guilty about that apparently were quite normal for a caregiver. I had a passing conversation with Coco, a friend and member of my church. She shared with me her experiences in being a caregiver for both her mother and her sister. She, too, had her challenges which are a natural part of being a caregiver. Not long after that, Marie N., one of my SAG sisters, asked me whether or not my husband had made me mad. My mouth dropped wide opened. Marie smiled and said that in time he would make me mad on more than one occasion and that it was OK. All this time, I thought that I was a hateful substandard wife. These feelings apparently were quite normal. I would often chuckle after my friend, Denise (Dunice Jean is her real name), would give me a call. She had been a caregiver for a daughter who died a few years ago. Denise would call and say, "I am just checking on the sick and the shut in. Rick is sick and you are shut in!" We would just laugh and then hang up and go our separate ways. Without talking to another caregiver I would have never known the difference. I found out that I was more than normal. What a relief!

Once while we were in Connecticut, there was the diarrhea explosion incident. I have a bit of a weak stomach, but somehow, I was able to leave my body for a bit of time, deal with the situation and then return to my body in a normal, if somewhat altered, state. For some reason my sister Ellouise and her nursing buddies found this scenario hysterical, and I guess in a weird sort of way it was. I am happy that I provided them with some comedic relief!

You just do what you have to do to handle what is on deck. Unless a person has walked in the shoes of a caregiver, they are unable to really help you understand these very specific dynamics.

Getting a Complete Physical

Now is a good time to contact your doctor and get a complete physical. You can be so involved with taking care of your loved one that you overlook your own basic medical care. Even if you don't think you need a complete physical, go and get one. There is truth to the old adage: The caregiver is the "first to go." In 2006, there was an excellent article in

the *Parade Magazine* that cited a study published recently in the New England Journal of Medicine. This study found that for people 65+ years, hospitalization of a spouse increases their risk of death up to two years. The effect varied according to the spouse's diagnosis. The study looked at the combined effect of the "caregiver burden", which links the effects of illness in one spouse to the risk of illness in a caregiver spouse. Listen to your body and take care of yourself no matter what is swirling around you. Not doing so not only risks your own health, but maybe your very life.

Depending on your level of stress, your doctor might recommend a mood elevator or something like that. I stayed away from this option and was able to work things out with my faith, Scream Buddies, mini trips, painting/drawing, or the gym. However, you and your doctor might consider another alternative.

Again, the Internet is your best source when you want to research any health issue you that might be troubling you. Much to your surprise, you will find out that while your issue may be unique to you, there is a boatload of information on the Internet on whatever is ailing you.

Sleep Like a Baby

Don't forget the importance of sleep. As stated before when someone has a newborn in the house, whether it is the dad or the mom, it was always sage advice to tell the new parents to sleep when the little one slept. This same advice rings true when you are a caregiver.

You are in a constant state of sleep deprivation and really don't even know it. Take a nap or lie down from time to time just to be able to hear yourself think. I also used a sound machine and go to bed each night listening to the ocean. Many of the wonderful trips that Rick and I took were to the ocean. There are other programmed sounds that you might like: rain, forest babbling brook, etc. Each type of sound machine has a variety of options.

Doth Thy Cup Runneth OVER?

Take a look at your life. Since we are in agreement that you are NOT a super hero, you should do an inventory of what you "have to do" and what you really NEED to do. I had to learn to say NO on more than one occasion. I had to take a leave of absence from my Sunday school teaching duties during Rick's illness because my full plate had turned into an overflowing platter.

My sister, Debbie, was by my side during Rick's illness and there the night of his death. Towards the end, Rick was extremely agitated during the night and had to be sedated every four hours. For some reason, he felt he needed to fix the trapeze on his bed. He would constantly beat the trapeze with his remote control. Needless to say, I was in a constant state of sleep deprivation. Debbie came over and spent nights so that I was able to go upstairs and get a good night's sleep. In the morning, she looked at me and shook her head and said she had no idea how I was able to do this night after night. I told her that you just do what you have to do.

Outside Interests

Make a point NOT to stop your outside interests. Try to continue doing what you have been doing within reason. You need an outlet. Doing something outside of the house will help refresh you and allow you to more effectively handle the stressors at home. These interests are a part of who you are. Not participating in what you love to do will make you resentful and steal your joy.

If you don't have any outside interests, find some:
- ☐ Check with your church.
- ☐ Volunteer at the school.
- ☐ Opt to baby-sit or dog-sit from time to time.
- ☐ Take a cooking class or knitting class.
  During the last six months of Rick's illness, I knitted four double-size afghans and seven baby afghans. He said that he loved to hear the clicking sounds of the needles. He found it quite soothing. It was a great balm for my nerves and I was able to create some heirloom gifts for my friends and their children.
- ☐ Sign up for an art class at the local community college.
- ☐ Take woodworking or auto mechanics.

☐ If you are one of the lone rangers that do not know how to operate a computer, there are many classes available to you, some of which are free. You can take these classes to increase your ability to surf the Internet and to create documents. The use of a computer will open up a whole new world for you.

Bowl, Book & Bottle (2005)

The key is to do something that will take you out of the house and away from your situation, if only for an hour or two. You will come back refreshed and invigorated. I enjoy painting. I started painting again, in earnest, when I retired. Ruth converted her garage to a wonderful painting studio and I would lug my junk down there and we would paint and eat and paint some more. This proved to be some of the best therapy that I have ever had. I also would paint a bit more when I got home. If you love painting like I do, you can lose yourself for hours in this medium. I even signed up for a painting and drawing class at the local community college. It has proved to be a wonderful release for me; I just need to do it a bit more.

Keeping a Journal

I personally would rather put hot needles in my eyes than to keep a daily journal. This would involve *SITTING STILL* and thinking. While this is not my cup of tea, I know for a fact that it is a wonderful outlet for so many

other people. To be honest, I must confess that when I actually did keep a journal, I really did like it. I found that a lot of the noise in my head wasn't there when I would commit my thoughts to paper. My sister, Ellouise, is a journal writing fool and swears by this concept.

I was blessed to have Coco G. in my life. She is the younger sister of a friend who died of breast cancer. Coco is one powerhouse of a woman and wrote a book entitled, *Journaling the Journey: The Power of Putting it in Writing!* It is a religiously oriented book that has practical principles for anyone and everyone. I strongly suggest that you consider this as an option. (See listing in Reference Section.)

Some folks like to keep a journal on their computer. That is fine if you are the only one that uses that computer. You might not want someone to read what you have written when you are really ticked off and having your own personal pity party that particular day.

However, I have now started using a simple spiral notebook to record some of my days. I have a lovely journal that was a present from Jake that is leather bound and really beautiful. This accompanies me when I travel and I log in my daily experiences in Iowa and other far away places.

"Run, Caregiver, Run"

Those who mean well tell you to simply get out of the house and do something. When you are a caregiver, trying to "get away" is a lot like having your right foot nailed down to the floor and then trying to run. No matter what you are doing, you are always tied back to the house. You will find yourself checking your watch or the clock wondering when the waiter will come and ask for the dessert order. You are "away," but not really. A person can only go so far with a nail in your right foot. You may also hear the tired response of, "Well, you married for better or for worse." Anyone who says this has never been a full-time caregiver. Again, the power of connecting with a support group that has members who have walked a mile in your shoes is immeasurable.

Go early and go often.

This sounds a bit weird, but you will need to take a break from time to time. I didn't realize that I was as tired as I was until my sister, Diane, insisted that I visit her in Texas for four days. Rick was recuperating from his back surgery and had not yet been diagnosed as terminal. I made arrangements for someone to look in on Rick and went to Austin, Texas. I had a ball, but slept almost 12 hours the first night I was there. I shopped and ate and then shopped some more. Rick was very happy that I had gone away for a few days and had daily treats and meals delivered to him from neighbors and friends. He also had 14 zillion phone calls from friends and family. When flying back, I was actually happy to be going home and excited to see Rick, and he was happy to see me. We both needed that break, and we didn't even know it.

My sister, Debbie, also kidnapped me in January 2006 and took me to San Diego for three days and two nights. I basically rested the first evening and just dealt with only my needs. I had a massage, ate good food and, of course, did some shopping. There is nothing like a little Retail Therapy! Again, when I came back home, I was rested, locked and loaded and ready for whatever was waiting for me. Rick was happy that I was back home and well rested.

My neighbor, Cindy, had a mother who died young of Multiple Sclerosis. Her father took care of her mother to the extent that he eventually had a severe heart attack due to stress. Cindy emphasized to me that I needed to go somewhere every 30 to 60 days to recuperate and rest. I wasn't able to exactly do that, but I did try to get away whenever it was possible. Even if it is for just a day or two, try to do this. You will return to your responsibilities rejuvenated. Check with your long-term health care organization or hospice to better understand your associated benefits for "respite care". Respite care is an identified need and is part of many of these programs.

Rick and I also took a few trips together. We went up to Sparks, Nevada to visit Don and Phyllis. It was great to be with them and have fun. We got up there between storms and saw the Sierra Nevada in its most beautiful winter wonderland attire. Rick also wanted to go back to New England to visit his family, particularly his children and grandchildren, and my sister Diane and her family. We flew back for a week and had a wonderful time. How he made this trip, as sick as he was, was nothing less than a miracle. His nurse said that it was sheer will power on his part to make it all the way across the country and back. To make this easier on Rick, I made wheelchair assistance requests for all of our connections and flew him back home first class.

Field Trips with Your Loved One

Since Rick was not able to drive anymore, I tried to think of field trips to take him on that he might enjoy. Two trips stand out in my mind.

- **Nimbus Fish Hatchery**: Earlier in Rick's diagnosis and prior to chemo taking the very life out of him, I took him out to see the fall salmon run at the Nimbus Fish Hatchery. Rick was an avid fisherman and enjoyed fishing for salmon. If there was a fish in the water, I tell you that man would catch it! He really enjoyed that day and we walked up and down beside the ladders watching those fish jump and swim up the ladders. It was exhilarating for both of us.

- **Costco:** Yes, Costco. Rick liked to go to the store because he didn't have to use his cane and could lean on the shopping cart while I tossed in groceries. When we drove up to Costco, I told him I bet they had those carts that you could drive. Well they did. It was so much fun to watch him take off driving a vehicle for the first time in eight months. He was like a little kid. The man was all over the store, going down all the aisles. I just smiled and watched the little orange flag on his scooter go up and down the many aisles. I went my way and later when he caught up to me, he had the biggest smile on his face. It was adorable.

Stop and take a moment or two to think about what would bring a smile to your loved one's face. There are also articles on happenings around town in the local weekend paper to give you additional thought starters. (Notice how much I use that phrase?)

Preserving Your Loved One's Dignity

This is a touchy subject, but one that I want to discuss with you. When people are gravely ill, they feel they are losing control of even the basics. When we try to do so much for them, we might inadvertently be squeezing them out of the picture. In my case, I handled the majority of the finances. There were a few bills that Rick would pay a couple of times a month. It would have been much easier for me to just take these over and pay them and relieve him of the task. Because I am fairly competent with the computer and the Internet, I paid almost 100% of the bills electronically. Electronic bill pay was always a quick and simple option for me.

Once, when I thought I was helping him, I paid his bills. I am on the account, so in my mind, it was no big deal. Well, it was to him. He insisted that I let him handle his own financial matters and that he wasn't so incapacitated that he couldn't do it. Oops. I found out that even when he was in La La Land due to the morphine he was taking, he still knew when his bills were due, the amounts, and when the automatic deposits were made into his bank account. He told me on more than one occasion not to count him out yet. He was planning to pay his June bills a week before he died and had his checkbook out to do so. I respected his wishes until the end.

Also, involve your loved one in any decision that you would normally discuss with him/her. Even though I knew that I would have to make the final decision regarding our finances or any projects at home, I always ran decisions past him for his approval. This is basic common courtesy, and it allowed him to keep his dignity in place. If it was a complex issue, I would type up the situation on a form and then check off the items when we had the discussion. I even did this when we discussed his funeral plans and burial. I took a business-like approach and removed a lot of the emotion from potentially volatile situations. You don't have to be a forms nut like me, but this is one way to handle it.

Visualize Your New Life

Well, it is true.

You will have another life if your spouse or loved one enters a nursing home, becomes further disabled or, sadly, dies. You want to be sensitive, but still need to start planning for your future. Consider planning a trip, redecorating a room, picking up a new hobby, volunteering, or going back to work

I am not telling you to bring in decorators, paint color swatches on the wall, or start measuring for new curtains in your loved one's sick room. However if you have a similar project, it will give you a reason to go out of the house and look around Home Depot, Lowes or a wallpaper store. Start a file or look at the Home and Garden Networks. This project will give you something to do that is far removed from your daily tasks and possibly tap your creative juices.

Towards the end of Rick's illness, I was urged by Cindy and my friend Diana to visualize traveling to some place where Rick and I had never been. Diana said that she wanted to plan a trip for me. I told her that I wanted to go to Greece and Turkey after Rick passed. She said "No problem" and that she would make all of the arrangements. We would talk from time to time and when a program came on TV that was about Greece, my ears would perk up with interest.

While I visualized this trip, out of respect, I never discussed it with Rick.

KEEPING YOUR SANITY
ACTION ITEMS

Done (X)	Item	Required Action	Status	Comments

Those Who Want to "Help"

"No one can get your goat, unless you tell them where it is tied up!"
African Proverb

This is a touchy subject. You will find people who really want to help and those who just want to just be in the mix. They want to help, but just don't know how. They also may be working out "stuff" that has occurred in their lives. Quite often people will give to others what they wish they had.

Let me clue you in on this one. If you really want to help, ask the caregiver what he or she needs and how you can help. This was a hard one for a former Wonder Woman. I felt really uncomfortable asking for help and didn't do it for several months. When I was admitted to the ER, the doctor counseled me to allow others to reach out and help me. He asked me if people had offered to help me. I said "yes", but I always said I was OK and declined the offer. He said that the next time people offered to do something for us; I should take them up on their offer. Debbie W. from St. Paul called me up and TOLD me she was bringing over a complete meal. She is one heck of a cook, and Rick and I were treated to a complete gourmet meal. Then the food flood gates opened up. Coco and Phyllis W. came with mountains of food and I didn't have to cook for almost three weeks. Guess what? I began to eat, and with each bite, I knew that I was loved and felt their wonderful support.

It is OK, Superman or Superwoman… ***sit down, be quiet and accept the help***. You won't diminish your super powers when you allow others the opportunity to feel that they are really helping you.

Now for those of you, who want to help a caregiver, don't let them off the hook. Tell them that you want to do something specific. People are "funny" about having others in their house. I know that I was. Think of something that people can do for you. It can be as simple as reading to your loved one or going to the store for you; picking up a prescription; bringing over some inspirational reading or music; washing your car; sweeping off the entryway. Bringing over a meal is always a safe bet and will be deeply appreciated by the family. I even had a couple of people bring over cases of bottled water. They are convenient for your patient, guests, and you.

Lunch or Dinner with Friends

During one week, I had the pleasure of having lunch or dinner with girlfriends four days in a row. Rick was resting most of the time; we had in-home care and he did not mind me taking time to see a friend or two. In fact, he encouraged these outings. I had a great time and had wonderful meals, yet felt more stressed after each event.

I had to stop and think why I was feeling this way. It then dawned on me. Although I was out having a fun time, the main topic was Rick, his health, and impending death. I was not able to escape from my caregiver responsibilities because I was reliving my on-going stress each time I met with them. When you relive stressors in your head or in a conversation, you are experiencing the same stresses over and over again.

To address this, I had to tell my friends that our visits were an opportunity for me to have a brief respite from my caregiver responsibilities. I gently told them that I didn't want to talk continually about Rick or his death. They understood and were very respectful of my request. I am sure that your friends will understand as well.

Those who rain on your parade: The Negative Nellies

They are out there and don't even know that they are Negative Nellies. They can bring you down, make you feel even more stressed or incompetent and generally set your hair on fire! I had one friend whom I truly love, but had to take in smaller doses during Rick's illness. Whenever I would go and visit, my friend would lower their voice, look deep into my eyes, touch my arm and say, *"Now, dear, how are YOU really feeling? What you are going through is an arduous journey and is so sad and it must make you feel very bad and overwhelmed. It is so horrible that this is happening to both of you."* Now I needed *that* type of "support" like a hole in my head. My friend did it a lot. When I mentioned to my friend that I felt worse after a visit, on the very next visit, my friend would then OVER correct the tone of the conversation and be so dat gum happy that I wanted to scream. My friend really didn't mean any harm, but at times I couldn't filter all of that emotional noise and chose to receive the support over the phone.

Unsolicited Medical Advice

Grrrrrrrrrrrrrrrrrrr... This is a slow burn....

Out of the blue, I had a few people who at the last minute called and suggested that we take an entirely different tack on Rick's treatment. They didn't want to interfere but then gave me a list of other options that we should consider. Now here he is... he has lost 86 pounds, is no longer eating, and I am offered a suggestion to give him a new experimental treatment in which his cells are harvested and tested for different types of chemo and then a decision could be made as to which one would help him. I was told to consider this option and to check out the validity of this option on the Internet. It was a bit late, don't ya think?! Others wanted him to try a holistic approach to his terminal cancer.

Did these people think that I WASN'T trying everything that I could to save Rick? This type of "help" will make your blood boil, unless you back away from it a bit. I was faithfully following Rick's wishes regarding his choice of treatment. They meant no harm and I tried not to take it personally. I first felt extremely incompetent when I was given these types of suggestions, but had to put it all in perspective. Those people simply felt helpless and were grasping at any straw they could find to try to save Rick.

This situation was particularly hard because Rick had taken a rather passive role in this entire process. Rick left *ALL* major decisions up to me. However, I would run these suggestions past him, and in all cases, he was not interested the least in any options other than traditional medical procedures—***Period***. He had accepted his fate and was comfortable with it.

 A strong suggestion is to identify the **TOXIC** people in your life at this time and minimize contact with them. Under other circumstances, you may be able to ward off these people. However, when you are in the middle of this nightmare, your defenses are down and you are like a turtle without its protective shell. During Rick's illness, I had a friend who had lost a loved one. This person was so unbelievably upset, but needed my assistance until other living arrangements could be obtained. In addition, I was listed as a Medic Alert system's "first responder" for another friend who had medical issues. On one occasion, I was called out three times during the early morning hours because the friend had fallen and could not get up. I found myself becoming anxious whenever I went to see either one of these beloved friends. After a bit, I realized that this high level of negativity was wearing me to an emotional frazzle and grinding me down to a stub. Between dealing with Rick's impending death and these added factors, I was getting negativity in triplicate. I had to back off a bit and limit my interaction with these friends and this alleviated my stress level tremendously. Learn to say "No" and pace yourself.

A toxic person may even be someone who is supposed to be very close to you and should have YOUR best interests and care in mind. I was told by one that they and "others" had issues with how I was taking care of Rick. They particularly didn't agree with my taking respite breaks from time to time. I became extremely upset and Rick could tell. When I shared these comments with him, he calmly said that they were not with us day and night and had no idea about the amount of associated stress that I was under. After choking a bit, I swallowed this bitter pill; but I emotionally kept them at arms' length during the remainder of the process.

People, let me give you a word of advice—if an inner voice says, "Maybe I shouldn't say this, but"—*THEN DON'T SAY IT!*   I don't care if the inner voice is Peter Rabbit, Krishna, Isis, the Holy Spirit, your personal Spirit Guide or Buddha, listen to it and keep your mouth shut!   The last thing that Rick needed right now was me hemorrhaging emotionally due to the fact that I had been deeply wounded by these inconsiderate, and basically cruel, comments. If someone starts the conversation with, "Maybe I shouldn't say this, but"—Stop them dead in their tracks and redirect this emotional missile. You should say, "NO, you probably shouldn't." In your mind say, "olé" and let this emotional "bull" trot right on by you.

You are under tremendous strain and pressure right now and your phasers or protective shields might malfunction and be in the locked-down position. So kindly put these toxic people on the back burner. *It is not necessary to grandstand and state why you are doing this, just do it to minimize the amount of emotional noise around you.*

These people care for your loved one and you, but may be grasping at straws in order to help in any way possible. They mean well… (I think)… Now let's all un-ball our fists!!

THOSE THAT WANT TO HELP
Action Items

Done (X)	Item	Required Action	Status	Comments

Disclosure of Illness

It is imperative that you fully understand the personality of your loved one when it comes time to disclose the nature of his or her illness.

I have a very "public" personality and when I walk into a room, I can suck the very air out of the room. While I am comfortable discussing almost anything with anyone, my husband was not. How to handle this situation was really quite simple—I asked him. At first, Rick only wanted people close to him to know what was going on, which I respected. However, as time went on, I explained to him that he was deeply loved and people wanted to "be there" for him and for me. He relented a bit. We were then floored by the out-pouring of love, affection, genuine care and support that we both received. However, your loved one might not feel this way at all, and you must be sensitive to their wishes regarding disclosing their illness.

Both of my parents, Beatrice and Harold Toney, died from cancer. My mother died at the tender age of 44 and my father at the age of 67. My sisters and I did not know the seriousness of our mother's cancer. She had had some "female" issues and had a hysterectomy. That was all we knew. The next thing I knew, I was receiving a call from my godfather saying that I needed to get home from college if I wanted to see my mother alive again! Then, she simply slipped into a coma and was gone in a few days. Talk about feeling emotionally short-sheeted! We didn't have any time to say goodbye or balance our emotional books with her prior to her death. Our father, on the other hand, knew he was dying of liver cancer. Since it wasn't a secret, we discussed his impending death and even had parties. Nothing was left unsaid. His death, although sad, had closure. My mother's death was an open wound that took years to close. Needless to say, I support some sort of ongoing disclosure of the nature of the illness to all concerned parties. Again, you must respect the wishes of your loved one in how much information they opt to disclose and when.

My son, daughter-in-law, and I were concerned about how our oldest grandson, Rodney III, whom we called "Punkin", would handle the impending death of his Papa. Punkin was extremely close to Rick or "Papa" as everyone called him. In fact, Punkin's first nickname was "Little Papa" because as a baby he looked so much like Rick. Rick, our assigned hospice social worker, and I decided that we would bring Punkin over on the social worker's assigned visitation day. She could explain Rick's impending death to Punkin. This had been previously cleared with his parents. When, I expressed my concern about Punkin and Papa to my sister, Diane, who is a librarian, she had recommended a book, entitled, *When Dinosaurs Die,* by Laurie Krasny Brown and Marc Brown. This is a great book that walks a child through the entire impending death process. Alex secured the book and all was set… or so we thought.

My daughter-in-law sat Punkin down prior to his visit and explained to him that there was a lady who visited Papa and talked to him about his health. This lady would like to talk to him about Papa's impending death. To our surprise, he put his foot down and said a firm "No!" He said that all he needed to know about death his Papa would tell him and he didn't need any lady to do it for him. So we arranged for Punkin to come over to visit his Papa. I left for a while and Rick sat down and read, *When Dinosaurs Die* to him and explained to him that he was dying. They discussed this with as much detail as they wanted. Next, they both went upstairs and played video games like they always had done.

What is important about this situation is that it was discussed. Any assumptions were put to rest because the affected parties, Punkin and Papa, addressed this delicate matter ***as opposed to a social worker and me.***

Rick was less forthcoming about his illness with other people, with the exception of a core group. We maintained this low level of communication until it was no longer practical.

A key in this entire process is to respect your loved one's wishes and preserve and keep your loved one's dignity intact. The sense of loss is so great for them in so many ways and the medical issues are intense. These are uncharted medical and emotional waters that you both must learn to navigate. I did everything I could to maintain Rick's level of dignity during this process and to protect his privacy.

Discuss the level of disclosure that is appropriate with your loved one and honor his/her wishes. But HAVE that discussion as soon as you can. Communicating throughout this entire process is important for both of you. On sensitive subjects, I found that I had to ease into certain matters by asking a vague question or two. I would then test the water to determine if I should proceed or address the matter at another time. You will reach a point where you will know how much information to disclosure and to whom.

DISCLOSURE OF ILLNESS
Action Items

Done (X)	Item	Required Action	Status	Comments

Hospice, the Angels of Mercy

"We are each others angels, we meet when it is time."

—Chuck Brodsky

Hospice personnel say they are not angels, but simply God's hands. I beg to differ. Where do I begin to tell you what Kaiser Hospice did for Rick and me? Until the day that they lower ME down, I will never stop singing the praises of Kaiser Hospice. Prior to Rick's illness, all I knew about hospice is that they came around to support the family just before death.

After Rick decided to stop chemotherapy, his doctor, with our urging, referred us to hospice. Rick was still somewhat hesitant about participating in the program. I was mentioning this to, Jake, my personal trainer and he in turn, mentioned it to Charley B., who also trained with Jake. Unbeknownst to me, Charley was a hospice volunteer. Charley came over to me and said that he knew what I was going through and asked if he could come over and speak to Rick about hospice. Charley came over one afternoon and we all sat around, drank tea, and talked for two hours. Appropriately, I said little and sat and knitted while they talked about the benefits of hospice. Charley is a kind and gentle man and walked Rick through the entire hospice process. What I didn't know, but found out later on, was that the only information that Rick had about hospice was about _residential_ facilities. He was adamant about not wanting to be sent away to an "institution" or placed in a nursing home. He wanted to die in the comfort of his own home. Once he found out that hospice could support the family unit

AT HOME, he said, "Sign me up!" This decision was the single most important thing that we did to handle Rick's illness and support our family unit.

To assist me in preparing for Rick's death, Charley gave me the book; *Final Gifts* by Maggie Callanan and Patricia Kelley *and Healing Elements of Design* a Healing Environment/Nightwood Publication. After reading *Final Gifts*, I was able to anticipate the various stages of Rick's impending death. My only regret was not reading it earlier in the process. I urge you to get this book and read it, if you are facing an impending death. I found it both insightful and extremely comforting.

Once Rick was diagnosed as terminal, the "waiting" period was waived for his long term healthcare coverage. I then contacted our long term care representative and she gave me a list of local organizations that would provide in-home health care. Being the control freak that I have admitted that I am, I was less than thrilled about having a bunch of strangers in our home. I prayed that God would point me in the right direction and help me select the appropriate company to help us. I liked the name of one of the organizations, "Visiting Angels." I felt that we needed all the angels that we could get surrounding us. When the doorbell rang, there was this petite Black woman standing there. I ushered her in and we sat on the couch. Karen H. simply smiled at me and said, "I know you. You and your husband attend St. Paul Baptist Church where I used to be a member." Call it what you want, but as for me and my home we know that God does indeed answer prayer. She was thorough and extremely professional and helped us get the type of personnel that best suited Rick's needs.

Within a day or so after making the decision to enter into the Kaiser Hospice program, an intake nurse visited us— then our case nurse, chaplain and social worker—and we were on our way. I cannot stress enough the importance of getting on board with hospice as soon as possible. They were a part of our support system for almost six months. I am saddened to hear about families who finally contact hospice only a short time before their loved one's death. It is a service that is a Medicare driven program that pays for a nurse, social worker, chaplain, limited in-home health care aid available and covered by most health plans. Please do your loved one(s) and yourself a favor and avail yourself of this wonderful program, or at least find out what the requirements are to participate in this program.

Our medical coverage was through Kaiser. They have a wonderful brochure that explains the program, entitled, "Hospice Program, A Guide to our Services." This brochure states:

"Hospice is a team approach providing care for patients facing the final stages of terminal illness. It enables the patient to live in dignity through symptom control, pain relief and emotional support. Death is viewed as a normal part of the life cycle."

Our Kaiser Hospice team had weekly meetings in their facility, in which each member discussed their portion of Rick's care. They shared notes and observations about what was occurring with Rick and with the family unit. These findings were then discussed with Rick's doctor. Any changes were discussed in the group format to ensure that everyone was on the same page regarding Rick's health.

Kaiser required the team to update a binder, which contained all of Rick's pertinent medical information and to have this binder placed in an obvious location. I would leave notes to a team member in their specific section of the binder to remind her of something or if I had a question. I would strongly suggest leaving a note because you might be (might be?.!!#@#$) a bit frazzled and might forget to ask a key question. I found the hospice personnel to be responsive to any message that I left them. There was also a 24-hour hospice hotline available to assist us any time after 5:00 PM. Whenever I had to make a call, a nurse would call me back immediately with medical advice.

This is a good spot to remind you of the importance of keeping a central calendar.

With so many people coming and going, a MUST HAVE is a central calendar in order to prevent double bookings, etc. This was particularly important when you have home health aides and your own medical appointments to consider.

OK, let me tell you about the roles and responsibilities of each hospice team member:

THE NURSE

Our assigned nurse worked very closely with Rick's doctor. She cared about Rick and was so tender with him. My husband, sweet as he could be, had a real stubborn streak and did not always want to color inside the lines when it came to his treatment. Well, "AttenTION"! When our nurse was in the house, there would be no nonsense. She was both firm and really funny. They would be laughing from time to time, sometimes when she had to do some sort of procedure that involved a dreaded suppository. Since he was terminal, there wasn't much of a point for him to have regular office visits. She would come by at least once a week to monitor his vitals, make any changes to his medications, and monitor his medical needs. Any changes or issues were discussed right away with his doctor. Our nurse had the private numbers of Rick's doctor and the pharmacy. You will have to check with your own medical plan to determine if you will be billed for prescriptions when your loved one is a member of the hospice program. All matters regarding his care were discussed with me at length. I was never left in the dark about any aspect of his care.

THE SOCIAL WORKER

Single-handedly, our social worker was one of the key people who kept me from going over the edge. She would come in and ask Rick how he was doing and whether there was anything that we might need. After the first meeting, she sensed the tension in the home. As stated earlier, she thought that she might know what might be happening and said that she would drop off some literature for  me to read. Rick had been in the military for 30 years and did two tours in Vietnam. He manifested the classic signs of PTSD. Retirement and a chronic illness can also bring these symptoms to the surface. Well, he had retired and was diagnosed with a terminal illness. While PTSD did not impact his medical condition, it did allow me to see that his withdrawal had nothing to do with him not loving me or not wanting to be married. Rick was totally consumed by PTSD and was clinically depressed. Once I found this out and did more research on my own, I un-balled my fists and set about trying to do everything that I could to make his final months as happy and stress-free as possible. I know in my heart that I was and will be eternally grateful to our social worker for lighting my path to understand the effects of PTSD.

Our social worker also keenly monitored **how I was doing**. Her experience let her know that without proper monitoring, the caregiver can bottom out in record time. Although Rick was dying, there was a large part of me that was also dying. Taking care of a loved one can be all-consuming and may prevent you from taking your own psychological temperature. Guard against this, or you might just be a heart attack or stroke waiting to happen. This wonderful woman would always inquire what I was doing for myself to release the tension. She encouraged me to take a few days here and there to go out of town so that I could get a good night's sleep. Although Rick strongly encouraged me to go away for a few days on two separate occasions, I caught holy hell in some camps for taking these brief respites. However, these two trips allowed me to deal with my sleep deprivation and come back more refreshed and better able to take care of Rick and to coordinate his care.

One of the benefits of the long-term health care that we had was a respite benefit. This provision had paid benefits for specific scheduled rest periods for the caregiver. Kaiser's Hospice program had similar benefits in which they would provide a person to be with the patient while the primary caregiver took a break. Each organization has a different set of requirements. You will have to find out about your specific benefit plan.

THE CHAPLAIN

Ah, the chaplain. We already had a spiritual advisor, our Pastor, Rev. Ephraim Williams of St. Paul Baptist Church, in Sacramento, California. So I wasn't too sure if we needed a chaplain, but I thought, why not, she came with the hospice package!

But our chaplain... what a joy! She was tall, really cool, hip, earthy, and played the Native American flute. I thought that *I* was direct, but I was a pantywaist compared to her. There would be times that she would come in towards the end and ask Rick, "Are you tired of all of this poking and prodding"?…"What'cha thinking about?" While on the surface one might think that she was a bit direct, Rick really responded well to her tender yet no-nonsense approach. Maybe this was a result of him having served 30 years in the military. She always got information from him regarding his spiritual state of mind that no one else could. Our chaplain was the one whom Rick told he had seen an angel at the bottom of his bed on three occasions and that after the third time, all fear of death left him. Later, when asked if he was ready to cross over, he would say, "No" or "Not yet" and then finally after one of the chaplain's visits, he said, "Yes and it will be soon."

Rick was half Native American (I won't tell you which half) and I believe that it was not a coincidence that she played the Native American flute. Sometimes she would come in and gently sit in a chair and play the beautiful songs that she composed. Even towards the end, when he spoke very little, I remember this special woman came into his sickroom and played the flute in almost total darkness. When she finished, he simply moaned and lifted his boney arm and waved in her direction. Our chaplain also honored Rick by playing the Native American flute at his memorial service.

The chaplain assigned to us had a non-denominational approach and spoke to his spirit and his body. So if you are concerned about any conflict with your spiritual or non-spiritual walk, I found that there was none. It is a natural aspect of death and dying that needs to be examined and discussed. After visiting with Rick, she would always go into the kitchen to touch base with me on where I was in the entire process.

I am convinced that it was not a coincidence that all three of these unique women were sent to us. They knew when he was at his final stage and kept me informed every step of the way. The advantage of hospice is that they have concentrated experience in dealing with death and dying and are able to coordinate their vast knowledge on all aspects of the rather unique experience called death.

If the health of your loved one begins to deteriorate, I strongly suggest that you find out all about the hospice benefits covered by your medical plan as soon as possible. Knowledge is power in this entire process. Armed with knowledge, you decrease the amount of stress that you have. I was organized and knowledgeable of all aspects of Rick's care, and still my hair fell out and I had lost 15 pounds by the time Rick actually died. Unfortunately, stress will be your companion throughout this entire process. Don't let anyone fool you in this regard.

Advanced Healthcare Directive – Do Not Resuscitate Order (DNR)

This is a tough one. You should discuss this concept early in the process. When we signed up with hospice, they explained the document to us, but Rick opted not to sign for a while A few months later, when it was no longer possible to ignore the obvious, Rick did sign the document and we put in his Kaiser Hospice binder. It was recommended that we post it on the front door. I opted not to do this because I didn't want my children or grandchildren to see the document. It was a really difficult process, but one that had to be put in place. Our nurse explained the physical aspects of what happens when you try to resuscitate a person and how it interferes with the body's natural course of action. Rick was dying and was not going to get any better. He wanted to die with dignity and grace. DNR was his wish and we followed his direction on this matter.

HOSPICE AND OTHER IN-HOME CARE
ACTION ITEMS

Done (X)	Item	Required Action	Status	Comments
	Is hospice covered by medical plan?			
	Discuss option with loved one			
	Determine is there is any spiritual conflict in having an assigned chaplain.			
	Set up a meeting with hospice personnel			
	Enroll in the program			

Celebrations of Life

"To every thing there is a season, and a time to every purpose under the heaven:

A time to be born, and a time to die; a time to plant,

and a time to pluck up that which is planted;

A time to kill, and a time to heal; a time to break down, and a time to build up;

A time to weep, and a time to laugh; a time to mourn, and a time to dance;

A time to cast away stones, and a time to gather stones together; a time to embrace,

and a time to refrain from embracing;

A time to get, and a time to lose; a time to keep, and a time to cast away;

A time to rend, and a time to sew; a time to keep silence, and a time to speak;

A time to love, and a time to hate; a time of war, and a time of peace."

Ecclesiastes 3:1-8
King James Version

Celebrations of Life

"You only have one life to live, and this is not a dress rehearsal!"

It is funny what I remember when I look back on the journey that Rick and I took prior to his transition to death. I remember once when he was able to walk around the grocery store by pushing the grocery cart and he came across some chocolate éclairs in the bakery section. He was a diabetic and said," Man I love éclairs, but I know that I shouldn't have them." I was incredulous; I looked him in the eye and said, "What are they gonna to do, 'Kill ya'?" He laughed and said "Good point." I told him to pick up two packages of the things. Even when he came across rib eye steaks, he said, "Good grief! These cost $12.00 each!" I leaned over and told him to buy four of them!

Anyone who knows me knows that I have an odd and somewhat off-beat sense of humor. I find humor in almost everything, and Rick and I did have our share of laughs during his illness. I remember once when he snapped at me, I told him that his outburst would cost him a demerit for the day. He said, "Fine, put me down for a dozen," and we both laughed.

Open House

Remember all of that support that we received when everyone found out that Rick had only six-12 months to live? While it was wonderful, at times it was also overwhelming. So many people wanted to come by and visit him or drop off a dish of food. While their intentions were honorable, he was growing increasingly weaker and the many visits made him extremely fatigued. In order to receive guests, his naps were interrupted and he would have to get dressed and then make conversation with his guests, etc. I then thought, "Hey, why not have one big Open House and everyone can come at once and visit with him for a couple of hours. I set up the date and time, sent out the information and decided to have cookies, tea and punch. This menu was simple and a hint that folks were supposed to visit for just a bit and not linger over the chicken wings and stuffed mushrooms and other standard open house fare.

We fully expected about 25 people to come on by and tip their hat to Mr. Rick. I had a nice little table set up with a sign-in book in which people could write down an expression or two. I got some balloons to mark the location of the house and settled down to meet and greet a few folks. Then they started arriving… precisely at 2:00 PM. In the door came Julius, then Bruno and Chenita, Denise and Aubrey, Alan and Doreen from the Sea Ranch, Kathy and Bill from the Redding area, members of the Usher Board, my Xerox cronies, my State of California friends, Rick's Fairfield buddies, our Bible study groups, our pastor and his wife, my son, Champy, our grandchildren and many other friends. Once I looked around, the house and the deck were packed with well wishers. The event went on until 5:30 PM and over 100 people had come to visit him and many called stating that they wanted to be there but couldn't. Some brought gifts and cards and tons of cookies. Rick was blown away by all of the people. He just sat in the chair and smiled and was overwhelmed by it all. Later that week, he would look at the sign-in book and just smiled as he flipped through the pages. This was more than either of us expected and he was so very happy… tired… but so unbelievably happy for this overwhelming outpouring of love and affection. Interestingly, several people came up to me at church and said that the open house was like a reverse baby shower. People take the time to plan and welcome someone new into the world; why not take the take to celebrate his life as he is about to exit the world?

What turned out to be something that I cooked up for practical reasons, ended up being a wonderful event and one of the sweetest memories of his final days.

An open house might be ideal for your loved one. You can tailor it to meet your particular needs and the medical condition of your loved one. A few simple alternatives might be barbeques, fish fries, and game nights, bowling events or whatever could prove to be a lasting memory for your entire family.

Tribute Book

AHHH…. the now internationally (well sort of) famous *Tribute Book.*

My daughter, Wendy, studied to be an events planner. She is a Type "A" personality who is organized to the nth degree. When Wendy received the news about Rick's cancer, she was devastated. She decided to take her angst and turn it into a treasure for Rick. Wendy had me send her a list of all of Rick's family and closest friends. She, in turn, asked them to put into words exactly what Rick meant to them and asked them to share their favorite 'Rick" stories. She collected all of these sentiments and treasured photos and created a Tribute Book for Rick Bailey. Wendy completed assembling the book and brought it up to Sacramento with her family during a visit after Thanksgiving. She presented it to Rick when he came into the kitchen. Rick took one look at it – looked up over his glasses, like Larry King – and said that he wanted to lie down and read it privately. Wendy and I went upstairs to gab.

When we came down for dessert, Rick was in his hospital bed sobbing uncontrollably. I went over to comfort him and all he said was, "I didn't know people felt this way about me. Bea, I just didn't know." Rick was reading the sentiments that Ruth wrote about him. Ruth said:

> "What a wonderful opportunity to focus on what the serendipitous events of our lives have created. All the things we have done, all the people we have met contribute to what I recognize as the fabric of our lives. Rick has become a part of the fabric of my life and I am a better person for it.
>
> First, let me say that the reason that Rick is woven into my fabric is largely because he is a person who would be more comfortable being a part of denim and flannel than silk and satin. At least that's how I see him. He's a blue denim; a durable, reliable, comfortable no-nonsense sort of fabric. Even though he would be more tolerant than I of the silk and satin people, Rick fits perfectly in my denim world. After all, blue

denim is strong, comfortable, dependable and preferred by most people. So is my friend Rick.

I count on all my denim clothes to be there. That's the cool thing about denim; it doesn't require a lot of maintenance. What matters is that it's always there to fill a wardrobe gap. I think about all the times when Rick could be counted on to be there. No flash or sparkle required. He would patiently be working with [Little] Rodney to improve his reading or videotaping Claire's wedding reception. Sometimes he shares his enthusiasm for world history and travel. More often he is counted on to satisfy our need for a fix to play Shanghai or LeRoy. But always, his participation is without fanfare. (Except for the times when he and Larry are insufferable because they are lucky at cards.)

As a man of faith, I am aware of the impact Rick has had in my life. Just the simple lessons of living his beliefs are apparent. It's never lost on me when we are out eating together that Rick will offer a blessing for our food. Because it's not a part of my practice, I'm maybe more conscious of it that I might be otherwise. But what I really get is that Rick lives and practices his faith. Its part of who he is and I have learned to see that who you become is rooted in what you do.

I'm pretty sure that God created denim so that we would always be comfortable and warm. I'm also pretty sure that God sent Rick to become a part of my fabric. I'm grateful for them both.

Love and kisses from Ruth"

By then, Wendy and I were now crying and we all were an emotional mess. We were so happy to be able to give Rick his "flowers" while he was alive and could still smell them.

The concept that I am trying to convey here is that you should look around and see what you can do so in the final chapter of your loved one's life so when you look back you will have few regrets. While it was hard for us to watch Rick slowly die with so much dignity and grace, we were fortunate to have had the time to prepare, as best we could, for his transition.

We know that not everyone has this "luxury" and your loved one might be taken from you in the blink of an eye. What to do? What to do?... Live each day as if it is your last one. Would I complain about Rick not putting the dishes in the dishwasher and instead putting them in the sink? (A uniquely male habit, I am told) ... I would not. Would I watch football with him as his beloved 2005 Oakland Raiders lost yet another game? ... I would indeed. Make your words kind and sweet and don't sweat the small stuff. Compared to death, it is all small stuff.

Saying Goodbye

In February, we decided to go to New England for Rick to say his final goodbyes to his family, and my sister, Diane, and her husband, Jerry and their children. He was determined to make this trip and was even able to play Trivial Pursuit with Diane and her family and some mean cards with his brother and sisters.

His sense of humor was still intact and you could hear his booming voice from time to time. His brother, George, and sisters, Linda, Judy, and Barbara, and brother-in-law, Jim, were so loving and kind towards him, and all told me how much they loved me and appreciated the care that I was giving to Rick. His daughter, Denise, came down from Vermont to say goodbye. She brought his grandsons, Ricky and Blake and her husband, John. My sister,

Diane, made Rick his favorite apple pie, and the final hugs from Diane, Jerry and Portia, their daughter, were gut-wrenching.

RJ, Rick's son, was his typical loving self and to this day calls me every Monday or Sunday evening to see how I am doing. No hidden agenda, just "Hey, Ma, how ya doing?" I don't know if he does this on his own or is keeping a promise he made to his father, but it is greatly appreciated.

Rick's family loves to play cards. During this visit, I was sitting at the table playing cards with his sister, Judy, Linda, Jim and Rick's niece, Sandi. Judy gently reached over while I was waiting for my turn, and started to gently pat and rub my hand. Nothing was said verbally, but so much was indeed said during this gesture. I was deeply moved by this act. Rick's brother, George, stopped me in the hall and took me by the shoulders, looked me in the eyes and told me to be strong and that he thanked me for taking care of his little brother.

Rick was happy to see them all. Regardless of his deteriorating health, he accomplished his mission to say a fond farewell to Barbara, Judy, George, Linda, Jim, RJ, Denise, John, Ricky, Blake, Jerry, Diane, Portia, Herb and the rest of his New England family. After his death, his nurse said that she had no idea how Rick was able physically make this trip. But, somehow he was able to do so. Although on a cane, he walked through the entire visit with his head held high and a faint smile on his face.

There were no tears…or at least none that he saw.

CELEBRATIONS OF LIFE
ACTION ITEMS

Done (X)	Item	Required Action	Status	Comments

Traditional Funeral Plans

"Though my soul may set in darkness,

It will rise in perfect light

I have loved the stars too fondly,

To be fearful of the night."

—*Sarah Williams*

Like it or not, none of us is going to get out of here alive, so avoiding making your final plans just doesn't make any sense. All of us have heard the horror stories about the mess that is left when there are no final plans to address the end of a person's life. There are family members who are not speaking today because Uncle John was buried in the blue suit and not the black pin striped suit and was buried next to Aunt Mabel and not in the military cemetery when "everybody" knew he wanted to be cremated and buried at sea.

The best thing that you can do for yourself and your family is to make your arrangements well in advance. If you do this in advance, your mind is clear and you are not operating under a cloud of emotions. By the way, have you made YOUR plans? The American culture (OK, here is my opinion) is so child-like when it comes to death. Newsflash—we are all going to die! Making these provisions will not speed up the process.

I completed the details for my death and burial about three months after Rick's death. I just about drove my children nuts and they thought that I was being morbid when I went into detail. While I had picked out the coffin I liked, I didn't like the black tuxedo trim because it looked too masculine. I made sure that Morgan and Jones would have the insert exchanged for a more feminine, yet tailored effect. I worried about what would happen after I died and how effectively they would use any inheritance I left them (hello... I would be dead... Ms. Control Freak... sorry kids [Nokie and Roy, too] for my madness). It is just when you are that close to all of this death stuff, it might make you a tad bit nutty while you are going through your process. But the funny thing is that when I had completed all of my arrangements—updated the trust, paid for the funeral, wrote up my final wishes, placed the disc of my memorial service program in my safety deposit box, and gave the key to my son—I was at peace... strange, but true. The kids were relieved that I now had something to talk about other than what color dress they should or should not put me in and how to style my hair. Why they didn't institutionalize me at this time, I will never know.

Making the Funeral or Memorial Arrangements

Discuss these plans with your loved one—in advance of any illness, if possible. If the loved one is not a planner, then you come up with a checklist or do the legwork for them and then tell them about it. Open casket, viewing of the body, buried here, in the home town, at sea, etc., are all categories that need to be discussed unless you want to end up with a really gnarly family mess on your hands. People are going to show their true colors and parts of their anatomy at this time; they generally do at weddings and funerals. Advanced preparation will cut "them" off at the pass.

When I was making Rick's arrangements prior to his death, I did my homework and put together an Excel checklist and sat down with him and checked off his responses. I had contacted the Veterans Administration and surfed the Internet. I kept the meeting short and to the point. The whole discussion took less than two minutes because I already was aware of some of the details.

Pre-Need Meeting

If the loved one was in the military, you need to get them pre-qualified for burial at a military cemetery. You can arrange this or the funeral home will do this during the Pre-Need meeting. I went up on the Internet and researched this area. My girlfriend, Ruth, who is my Scream Buddy, my ballast, and mainstay, went with me to the funeral home when I made Rick's pre-need arrangements. Even though I had my list (have you ever known me to be without a list?), I was surprisingly nervous. I knew what he wanted, because I had discussed it with him and I *DID* have a checklist after all. Yet, there was a lump forming in my throat and tenseness in my chest because this burial process was becoming way too real and was no longer theoretical. The flood of emotions in making these arrangements went way beyond a check list.

We completed the pre-need arrangements and put everything in place with a couple of humorous moments. During the arrangements, the funeral director had to step out for a moment when a really loud doorbell rang. I looked at Ruth and said "Good grief, that bell could wake the dead!" Next, the funeral director asked me if I would like to see the military coffin that I had picked out for Rick. I looked at Ruth and then back at the director and hesitantly said yes, unless there was someone in it! We all had a good laugh during this very trying time. Sometimes, laughter is the best medicine.

As stated earlier in this book, http//www.funeralwithlove.com/funeral.htm is a phenomenal website that is a storehouse of valuable information. This site even has a Funeral Calculator which you can use to enter information and get a good guesstimate on proposed costs. It discusses the different types of services and variations. I would suggest that you visit this site.

Obituary

Since you took my direction, you already have your obituary done, right? No one knows you like you know you. Waiting until the last minute to throw together an obituary only adds to the stress of the entire situation. Do your children know where you went to school or what you think were the high points of your life? Probably not. Again this is another action that could take some of the stress out of the situation. I wrote up my obituary, and when I kick the bucket, my children can add to it, but the core elements are there for them. I have a daughter who is very sensitive and expressive and a son who is in law enforcement and has a no-nonsense "give-me-the-facts" approach to a situation. They would have two distinct approaches to this subject matter. I have taken the mystery and some of the angst out of this process by writing down what I, (did I say **"I"**) want as part of my final plans. (*Kids, don't make me get up out of this coffin!*)

Another point I would like to make is that it costs MONEY to have an obituary printed in the paper. Many people think that this was a free public service. It is not. If you include a photo, for example, the cost in the Sacramento Bee was $55.00 and then an additional $2.65 for *each 17 characters*. Since this includes spaces and periods, the cost of your obituary can add up quickly. The obituary that I sent to the Bee cost me approximately $400.00. So if you opt to have the obituary printed in the local paper, choose your words carefully.

One thing that you can do is to e-mail the obituary to the paper in advance and they will tell you the cost for the document as it is written. You can then make any revisions by e-mail and they will give you an updated estimate. Once you get over the initial sticker shock, you now be able to make an informed decision on the length of the obituary. Also, most word processing software packages have a tool that will count the characters on a document so that you will know in advance the number of characters you have used. I was able to handle the entire transaction with e-mail, another method to relieve stress at this time. I had everything in draft form and when the sad time came, I only had to add the actual date of death, a few other details and email the document. I used a credit card to pay for this service and had completed this task in a matter of a few minutes.

One area of caution is using your loved ones actual date and place of birth and location/time of memorial in the printed obituary. It is possible that too much information can lead to identity theft, fraud and possible burglary during the memorial or funeral services. While this may not happen often, this is a reality of the world in which we are currently living and bears consideration when you compose a detailed obituary.

Funeral Calculations

Cremation or traditional burial? Sometimes the actual cost will help you make this determination. (*See Funeral Calculations Matrix in the back of this section*) In some case, there might be religious overlays regarding which concept is preferred. You want to get this matter clarified early on because there are no "do-over" if you inadvertently opt for cremation over a traditional burial!

Local Mortuary

Again, this is where the pre-need meeting with the funeral home is important. You can research funeral information on the Internet and be able to go into these meetings armed with relevant information and be in a better position to make informed decisions. *There is no charge for this pre-need service.*

I found a curious point with regard to cremation. Did you know that there are TWO different types of urns that are used for a cremation? One is designed to be opened when you are opting to spread the loved one's ashes, and the other is permanently sealed. I learned about this from a friend who had assembled with siblings to solemnly spread their mother's ashes in her favorite spot. However, this touching moment was marred because they had inadvertently selected an urn that was permanently sealed. They ended up using a brick and a tire iron to break open the urn. Not the most dignified or tender way to handle this situation.

Coroner's Office in Your Area

A lot of really good information can be found on the coroner's local web site. If you don't have access to a computer, you can give them a call or use the computer at the local library or copy shop to research this subject.

Internet

In researching this matter on the Internet, I came across a couple of really good sites that discuss general funeral planning information. One of these sites is http://endoflifecare.tripod.com/Caregiving

Payment Options

Good information on funeral insurance can be found on web sites like:

http://www.cbs.state.or.us/ins/publications/consumer/3932.pdf

http://www.moneymadeclear.fsa.gov.uk/pdfs/funeral-plans.pdf

Funeral Insurance can pay for your services at today's prices and not be impacted by future inflation. Another key point is that many plans allow you to change your mind from a standard burial to a cremation prior to your death. You, not your family members, can make subsequent changes to your original plans. There may or may not be costs associated with these changes. Kindly do your homework and determine which option is best for you.

A separate burial fund can be set up to also cover these costs if you opt not to use funeral insurance. Another suggestion is to make your payment with a **credit card** so that you have the backing of the company behind you if things don't go exactly as planned. Check with your credit card company to find out more about the details on how they resolve conflicts.

The funeral home may just ask to see a copy of your **insurance policy** to demonstrate the ability to pay when the time comes, if you are using these funds to pay for the arrangements. Again, the pre-need meeting will iron out these details.

What you ultimately do is totally a personal decision and I am not recommending any specific option. I am only encouraging you to look into these matters ahead of time

Required Documents

There are some important documents that you need to have in order to handle your financial affairs after your loved one has died. Now is a good time to gather these documents and place them in a secure location. Make your copies in advance. Please note that some organizations may require an original or certified copy of a birth certificate or a marriage license. If you don't have some of these documents, you will have sufficient time to acquire them from the appropriate departments.

Some of the documents are:

- o **Birth Certificate of the Deceased**
- o **Birth Certificate of Minor Children**
- o **Marriage License**
- o **Prior Marriage Licenses**
- o **Divorce Decrees**
- o **Social Security Card**
- o **Recent Photograph**
- o **DD214 Military Retirement Document**
- o **Life Insurance Policy**

If you are not able to locate these documents, you will be able to send for these documents with proper planning, in a non-crisis mode. Being the organized demon that I am, I had dividers within my file folder that had the subheadings listed above. By filing the documents in this folder, I was able to easily have these at my fingertips. Even with these systems in place, when Rick actually died, I was a mess and was more rattled than I had anticipated. I would have been lost without these devices to keep me on track and allow myself to navigate through this unknown process. Having all of this documentation available did a world of good for my nerves.

Arrangements with Your Religious or Social Organization

Again, prior to the passing of your loved one, you should contact the administrator or pastor, rabbi, priest, or whoever is appropriate regarding your loved one's and your desires for this final service. It is up to you both to set the tone of the service and the location. If your loved one never attended church, why on earth would you drag him or her into YOUR church for some religious ceremony that they would have never attended willingly, if they were alive? Because it makes you feel good? A service at the mortuary, social hall or at the graveside may be more appropriate. A prior discussion, if the situation allows it, will direct your course of action.

If you opt to have a **Repast** (a meal after the service), you have to let the facility know how many people will be attending. Our church does not charge members for this service and the food and beverages are included as a courtesy to its members. If you want to serve alcohol or spirits, your church may not authorize this and you might want to consider another location. Generally, the facility needs a week or two notice in order to prepare the food, but check with them regarding their individual requirements.

If you want to have a formal program during the repast, that will have to be decided. If you are going to have music, who will perform it? Will it be live, recorded or what? These details need to be determined in advance. If there are any costs associated with this function, you need to know what they are so that you have time to adjust your plans one way or another.

Housing Arrangements

This is an area that I researched prior to Rick's death because he comes from a large family and I was unsure of how many people would be attending his memorial service.

Obviously, the size of your home will be a factor as well as your relationship with your blended families. If your sister, Hortense, or your brother, Bubba, works your nerves, they might not be ones who should be staying with you at this stressful time.

I contacted several hotels in the immediate area and obtained various rates. Some of these hotels even had **bereavement discounts.** Once you find out the number coming, you can make whatever arrangements you deem appropriate. _Now who pays what might be another matter._ You might have friends who have a guest room who say that they would like to help you with arrangements. If you feel comfortable, take them up on their offers. Caution; have a clear understanding on this matter before the "fit hits the shan." This could be a landmine waiting to be detonated.

Memorial Program

OK, I created an intricate program booklet, but a simple page or two will serve the same purpose. The program I created was a labor of love and I started on it six months before Rick died. I had the "luxury" of time in this regard.

Depending on how involved your family member or friend wants to be, you can create a memorial program, if they opt for one, in advance and together. Rick did not want to be involved, so I did it. I am comfortable with the computer and creating a memorial booklet for him was a good release for my nerves. It turned out to be a special booklet with six pages of chronological family photos and poems and pictures of our many vacations. I know that he would have been proud of the final document. In fact, he told me so in a dream I had a few weeks after his burial. Most funeral homes will also prepare a simple program as part of their service package. They may also provide you with thank you cards. I tried to get my cards written immediately less this acknowledgement gets lost in the shuffle.

Whenever I attended a funeral and saw a program that I liked, I filed it away in a specific folder. During his illness, I received a lot of motivational poems and cards. If I saw something that I liked, I cut it out or tucked it into the Memorial Service Folder I had on my desk. So when it was time for me to start working on the program, these items were already in a single location. (Are you sick of me yet?)

There are honorariums or monies that are to be paid to a person singing, playing for a service or fulfilling another portion of the service. Some of the program participants may refuse. However, the proper protocol is to offer to pay for their services. When Brenda sang for Rick's service, I offered her an honorarium but she refused to take it. I, in turn, donated this money to a Memorial Fund I had set up in Rick's name to support the Dr. Ephraim Williams Family Life Center. I suggest that you give these envelopes to someone else to distribute for you before or after the service. You will have enough on your mind as you try to get through the service. Contact the administrator of your religious site or lodge to find out what is the standard payment and have the amounts ready the day of the service in separate envelopes.

Flowers or no flowers is a decision that needs to be made in advance. I selected Rick's flowers in advance and when Rick died all I had to do was make a call to the florist because the order was already on file. We selected a family wreath for Rick, and I asked anyone else to please make a donation to the Dr. Ephraim Williams Family Life Center, in lieu of sending flowers, which many people did. This request was also included in his obituary in the local paper and announced during church services prior to the memorial service. Several people still opted to send flowers anyway. Their acts of kindness were also appreciated.

Another option is making a donation in your loved one's name to your hospice organization. Many of the books and pamphlets given to family are the result of a donation. Your efforts in this regard would be greatly appreciated by your hospice organization.

FUNERAL COSTS AND GUIDELINES

Done (X)	Item	Required Action	Status	Comments

MEMORIAL Program
ACTION ITEMS

Done (X)	Item	Program Participant Phone Number	Cost	Comments

LEGAL AND FINANCIAL
CONTACTS

Name	Relationship to Patient	Phone Numbers Home, Work, Cell	Comments

FUNERAL OR MEMORIAL
ACTION ITEMS

Category	Contact Name	Address	Phone Number	Costs	Comments

Remembrances for Family Members and Friends

"As we grow up, we learn that even the one person

that wasn't supposed to ever let you down probably will.

You will have your heart broken probably more than once and it's harder every time.

You'll break hearts too, so remember how it felt when yours was broken.

You'll fight with your best friend.

You'll blame a new love for things an old one did.

You'll cry because time is passing too fast, and you'll eventually lose someone you love.

So take too many pictures, laugh too much and love like you've never

been hurt because every sixty seconds you spend upset is a minute of

happiness you'll never get back."

—Author Unknown

One of the regrets that **I** had was not making a video or audiotape for Rick's children, my children and our grandchildren. **I** wanted to do this, but he was not interested in this project. If it were **ME**, the Big Communicator (**I** didn't say a Great Communicator), **I** would have loved for Rick to have done this. *But, it wasn't me* and as **I** told him, this was his dance and **I** was responsible for the party favors, snacks and the music—a background artist in his personal symphony.

Nevertheless, making a video is a wonderful concept that could possibly help with the necessary healing that is required after the death of your loved one. Other options are:

- Individual letters to family members and friends
- Audiotapes
- Special trips to a favorite location or to a place that your loved one always wanted to visit.
- A meal at his/her favorite restaurant
- A specific night at home with family and friends
- Putting a scrapbook together
- Completing one of those journals that are directed specifically towards a grandchild from the grandparent. They can be purchased at almost any bookstore.
- Collecting favorite things that you and other members of your family want to bury with your loved one.
- Personalizing a stuffed animal by recording your voice inside of them. This is an option that would bring a tremendous amount of comfort to a child.
- A friend of mine told me that while his daughter-in-law was terminal, she purchased birthday cards and gifts for her children's future birthdays up to their 18th birthday. Her children currently are only eight and ten. What a phenomenal act of kindness and caring on the part of this valiant mother. She will be able to reach out from the grave for the next ten years to demonstrate her love to her children.

A myriad of emotions will surface during this entire process and not all of them are noble. This may sound morbid to you, but here are a couple of points you might want to consider:

- If you are bequeathing something, you should include it in the trust or will. This will eliminate some heated discussions and many hurt feelings. If there is someone who you want to carry out your loved ones wishes, they should be present in any discussions regarding inheritance. If there are any changes later on, everyone would be on the same page. Your loved one's wishes have to be written down, notarized and placed in a key location, such as your safety deposit box, given to your attorney, or given to the executor of your estate. Without proper documentation, any claims will be analogous to chasing smoke.

- Another option is to place labels on the backs of household items if you want specific people to have certain items. You should let your family know in advance that you have done this or at least tell a friend who can communicate your wishes to your family. Of course, if you have family members who are turning over pictures and looking for labels under the couch, you might need to be reading another type of book because there are larger issues at play here.

I think you get my drift. The key again is to talk about this with your entire family and make an effort to create lasting positive memories. Also, you don't have to do only one thing. If you have the time and your friend or family member is up to it, you could plan something every month, engaging in the more strenuous activities earlier in the process.

REMEMBRANCES FOR FAMILY MEMBERS AND FRIENDS
ACTION ITEMS

Done (X)	Item	Required Action	Status	Comments

Death of a Loved One

*"I am standing upon the seashore. A ship at my side spreads her white sails to the morning
breeze and starts for the blue ocean. She is an object of beauty and strength.
I stand and watch her until at length she hangs like a speck of white cloud
just where the sea and sky come to mingle with each other.*

Then someone at my side says: "There, she is gone!"

"Gone where?"

*Gone from my sight. That is all.
She is just as large in mast and hull and spar as she was when
she left my side and she is just as able to bear
her load of living freight to her destined port.*

*Her diminished size is in me, not in her. And just at the moment when someone at my side
says: "There, she is gone!" there are other eyes that watch her coming and
other voices ready to take up the glad shout: "Here she comes!"*

And this is dying.

—*Henry Van Dyke*

Death of a Loved One

OK, when I was in the process of writing this section of this book, I knew that it would be a difficult one. Nonetheless, I would set aside specific times to complete this section and invariably "something" always came up that prevented me from sitting down to write this chapter. The following important tasks prevented me from immediately writing this chapter of the book:

❖ *I needed to rake the leaves in the hidden hollow space near a crawl space by my deck.*

❖ *I needed to clean out my files from last year and shred documents.*

❖ *I needed to clean out my closet.*

❖ *I needed to rearrange the CDs and DVDs that I didn't even watch.*

❖ *I needed to take a nap.*

❖ *I needed to clean out the garage.*

❖ *I needed to take another nap.*

❖ *I should plant more roses in areas where they don't thrive and put in some bulbs where there was absolutely no sunlight.*

❖ *I needed to take a nap.*

❖ *I had to clean the individual leaves of my silk plants in a room I seldom used.*

Well, when I got down to "having" to clean my silk plants, I could no longer deny my avoidance behavior. In order to write this chapter, I had to swallow hard and relive a lot of the pain associated with Rick's death… sigh.

While I was going through this dying process with Rick, my beautician, Carla of Inner Beauty Salon, said something to me that was so accurate. She told me that *I can prepare all I want for Rick's death, but that I could NEVER get ready for it.* Unless you have gone through this, you will never know how accurate a statement this was. I had my lists, forms, packages, etc. and still I was in an emotional tailspin. I look back on it all and know that being as organized as I was did help bring some order in this sea of chaos. Simply doing half of the suggestions that I am offering will help you to navigate through this process in a more effective manner. Nevertheless, the experience will still hit you hard.

Preparation

Select Burial Clothes In Advance

Rick had decided on a traditional funeral. When he was in his final stages, I went upstairs and selected his suit, tie and shirt in which he would be buried. I put them into a suit bag and put the bag on a hook in the front entryway. Rick also wore dentures and used a specific type of hair product for his beautiful naturally curly hair. I put them together in a container and placed that near the front door. I knew that I would not be in any condition to select these items when his death actually occurred. I was able to select a shirt and tie that complimented his coloring. When the mortuary personnel came for him, they only had to take the items I had placed on the hallway hook. There was minimal involvement on my part, which was good because I was in no mental state to handle this matter.

This is also a good time to query family and friends in the event that they have a special object that they would like to bury with your loved one. This is particularly comforting to young children. Gather them together and give them to your mortician or have them ready at the gravesite.

Nut Box

Put together a **"Nut Box"**. I got this term from Marchand, who was a neighbor of mine who, at the time, had recently lost her husband. She was running in circles after her husband died. I told her to put key items in one container so that she would know where things were. She used an old tool box and she called it her "nut box." Depending on your organization level, you might want to start assembling these items in advance in case you have to order certified copies of birth certificates or marriage licenses.

The following chart lists some of the items that you might want to place in your own "nut box":

NUT BOX

Done (X)	Item	Status
	Key contact phone list for family members	
	Social Security cards	
	Marriage license	
	Medical personnel contact numbers	
	Safety deposit keys	
	Extra Set of house keys	
	Obituary	
	Extra set of car keys	
	Insurance Policies	
	Mock-up of funeral program	
	Loved one's wallet	
	Birth certificate, yours and your spouse's, if you are married.	
	Loved one's car keys with work keys and etc.	
	Security badge and or keys from work, if appropriate	

Stages of Death

Unless your loved one dies unexpectedly, there are key stages of death. Depending on the nature of the illness, they might linger in one area longer than another or quickly transition to the other side. Again, I would strongly suggest that you read the book, *Final Gifts* by Maggie Callanan and Patricia Kelley. These collections of stories and observations are extremely insightful, regardless of your religious persuasion. The back cover of this book states what the book covers:

"When someone we love is dying...it's hard to know how to help, what to do, what to say. Yet if we know how to listen and what to look for, the dying themselves can often supply the answers..."

I read this book a couple of months before Rick died. In retrospect, I wished that I had read it earlier. It would have given me some key insights into what was happening. You should read this book and share it with others in your family. It is not a sad book but one that provides you with insight and encouragement. It relieved a lot of my fears regarding his death.

There are specific medical stages that occur when a person is in the final stages of death. Again, hospice was instrumental in providing us with information. This information was given to us by our hospice nurse at the beginning, and even more detailed information was provided at the very end. The timetables listed are flexible and will vary from person to person. How the person is really feeling may not be shared with those who are doing the care giving. I cannot stress enough that during these final stages; you must do all that you can to keep your loved one's dignity in tact.

There are medical books that will give you in depth medical details regarding death and dying. You can obtain this type of detailed information from your health professional. However, there are some specific phases of Rick's dying process that I would like to share with you, in order to help you anticipate them as best you can. They were as follows:

Separation

During this one to two month period, Rick had a quiet knowledge that he was in fact dying and begin to withdraw from normal activities. Rick was never a big talker, but during this stage, his conversation began to decrease dramatically. I would talk to him, but most of the time he would give me short responses or merely nod his head. One day, he took his wedding ring off his boney finger and looked me in the eye. He said nothing, but gently pushed it towards me. I leaned down, took the ring, kissed him and said nothing.

During this time, his PTSD went into overdrive and he became clinically depressed and even more non-communicative. This was a painfully lonely time for me and I was overcome with a combination of sadness and helplessness. He spent most of his time asleep or in a twilight state with the History Channel quietly on in the background. During this phase, you have to respect the patient's feelings regarding company and the amount of stimulation that is around him/her. We had to change health care workers for this very reason. The aide that was assigned to us initially was very efficient and taught me a lot about caring for Rick's physical needs, but she was very high energy and extremely loud. This was a touchy situation, but was one that I had to step up to for Rick's sake. Her behavior was vexing to Rick as he was preparing his transition to another life. I discussed this matter with the agency and we had the person replaced with a low-key sensitive young woman who was soft-spoken. Rick found LaCressia to be quite soothing and attentive to his needs.

As I discussed earlier, Rick did not want a lot of people visiting him. As a result, we had the open house. However, there were times when I would simply take a message for him and not burden him with having to rev up and talk to a lot of people. It takes a great amount of energy for your loved one to focus on their dying process. Trying to entertain the caring people who would come by to visit was just too much for him at times. He had three close male friends, Dave B., Aubrey and Bruno. These gentle giants would come by to visit Rick, with a book in hand, and just sit by his bedside and talk whenever he wanted to talk or quietly read to themselves if Rick was sleeping. Dave came down from Idaho for two weeks during the Christmas holidays. Rick and Dave always talked about the current football happenings. Rick was pretty sick at this time and not very conversant, but Dave was content to sip his Pepsi as they quietly watched two separate Monday Night Football games. I don't think that more than 10 words were said during both visits. True friends don't require a lot of conversation.

My daughter and son-in-law, with grandson in tow, would often fly up from Los Angeles to visit Rick. He was active during the early visits, but towards the end was not able to interact. Rick was just happy to hear them bumping and thumbing around in the house. On several occasions near the end, I found my son-in-law, Roy, quietly sitting in Rick's sick room watching the History Channel like he and Rick used to do on so many occasions only Rick was in a deep sleep. It was extremely touching scene to observe them and I sadly smiled and said nothing to either one.

On several occasions, my son and daughter-in-law would come by and bring the three boys. Early on Punkin and Isaac would be crawling on Rick, and Maxwell would be swinging from the trapeze on Rick's hospital bed, or lying in bed with him. Towards the end, they would come to visit and just sit on the floor next to his bed and watch TV. It was so touching to watch their tenderness with Rick and he was aware and happy that they were there, even though at times he was limited in his interaction with them.

Rick's children and siblings would call from time to time, but he was unable to say much except to acknowledge the calls, say thank you, and to tell them that he loved them all.

At times towards the end, however, the grandchildren were frightened because their Papa was having hallucinations due to the medication he was taking for pain. We monitored his activities and limited the children's visits to times when he was more lucid. Our granddaughter from Tacoma, WA would come to visit. Sascha was older than the other children and was full aware of what was happening. She was saddened to see her Papa bedridden and helpless. He still tried to use his booming baritone voice whenever she was around to let her know that he was OK, but she knew that he was slipping away from all of us.

Food – If you are a wife and mother, you know you are conditioned to feed the sick and nourish them back to good health. Their not eating can be a source of real frustration and confusion. Food is not relevant to a dying person. Rick, who always had a lusty appetite, began to not eat. At times, he would have a "taste" for something and I would run out and get it or make it. He would then take a bite or two and that was it. Nothing stimulated his appetite and the food seemed to have lost its taste. However, on one occasion, he asked for a two-piece Kentucky Fried Chicken dinner with all the trimmings. Off I went to honor this request, and, much to my surprise, he ate every bit of this meal. At the end of his life, he only drank two eight-ounce glasses of orange juice a day for about three weeks. The energy that the dying requires is more spiritual in nature. They need spiritual food now and not your meatloaf.

Confusion

Although your loved one will be sleeping a lot now, there are distinct periods of disorientation. If he or she is on strong painkillers, these medications can and will have other side affects other than disorientation. If they are extremely pronounced, discuss this with your nurse and the medication can be adjusted. The patient is literally walking between two distinct worlds one to two weeks prior to death. I had often heard of the expression that the dying will be "picking" at their covers. I didn't know what that meant until I witnessed it. There is a non-stop restlessness and thrashing about and people do in fact "pick at the covers." There may be some congestion and coughing that occurs as the body begins to shut down. When Rick was diagnosed with lung cancer, my biggest fear was that he would be in excruciating pain, yelling out in pain, and that I wouldn't know what to do. He had none of these symptoms and, in fact, only had severe pain during the last couple of days. Rick's pain was handled by moderate use of drugs and a massive amount of prayer.

Invisible Visitors – This concept is not part of a Twilight Zone episode. It does occur more often than you might think. These reactions are a result of changes in the body and could impact the oxygen circulation to the brain. Another reason might be that there are, in fact, visitors in the room that the patient might see, but we are unable to see. Beware of this, and do not contradict or argue with your loved one regarding who or what they have seen or are seeing. It will only add to their confusion and yours and will ultimately frustrate you both. Rick had distinct visitors from the other side.

1). He told the chaplain and me that during his chemotherapy treatment, he was in his hospital bed and felt a small hand softly patting his hand as he lay in a twilight state. He said that initially he thought it was me, but then heard me upstairs. When the chaplain asked him who it was, he calmly said that it was his mother. She had come to comfort him.

2). On three separate occasions, he said that there was a man at the foot of his bed who said nothing. After the man's third visit, Rick said that all fear of death then left him completely.

3) One afternoon he asked me where the little boy was who was on the bed. I told him I didn't know (because there was no one on the bed). Later he asked about the little boy again. However, after reading *Final Gifts,* I knew to ask him who the little boy was. He said that the little boy was Isaac, our next-to-the-oldest grandson. Isaac was close to his

"Papa" and really liked Rick's hospital bed. In fact, when he wasn't too sick, Rick would get out of the hospital bed if he knew Isaac was coming over for a visit. Isaac would climb in the bed and work the bed controls. Isaac would ask me for a snack because, like Papa, his back hurt. He said that I should just stand there in case he might need something else from me. When my son observed this, he told Isaac that "Mimi" had worked to do and that he should not bother me. I then told my son that whenever Isaac around, attending to Isaac's needs WAS my work.

4). On one night, Rick sat up in bed, pointed to a TV tray, and said to me that that table needed to be on the 807 Manifest to the Philippines and I needed to make sure that it made it. Rick used to be in charge of transportation terminals in the Air Force and was responsible for moving both personnel and equipment. Had I read *Final Gifts* earlier, I would have known to ask him, "What time is the plane supposed to leave?" The dying knows when they are going to leave. Our caregiver, LaCressia, used to always say to Rick, "See you tomorrow, Mr. Bailey." He would always say, "OK, see you." Prior to his death, he quietly said to LaCressia, "No…no… you won't. I won't be here tomorrow." The next day he slipped into a coma.

Prior to the Actual Death of a Loved One

This stage varies, like all of the stages listed, from person to person. Rick and I talked about his impending death. I would say to him, "Honey, are you trying to leave me"? He would say, "Yes, but not yet." I would ask him if he trying to make me fall in love with him all over again. He would tell me that it was too late and that I had already done so. I would go to smooth his covers and he  would reach up and kiss me on my arm with his lips. I would playfully call him a "dirty old man" and he would smile. Rick was not anxious prior to his death. I asked him if he ever cried. He said that he did, but he had to be strong for me and the kids. I told him he did not have to be strong but, he firmly disagreed with me. Rick said when the question, "Why me?" came into his head, he would answer it by saying, "Why *not* me?" He had accepted his fate with a quiet dignity and grace that surpassed any level of my understanding.

Don't be surprised if your loved one has a sudden burst of energy and is far more communicative. Rick had been extremely quiet and had asked that the television be turned off and the room darkened. He did not want any company except the grandchildren and my adult children. He seldom took his phone calls and everyone understood. Once when I was puttering in his area, he quietly said to me, "Bea, you kept your word." I was puzzled by this and asked him what he meant. He said, "You kept me at home and didn't send me away." I was thunderstruck. Rick's fear was that once he became really sick, I wouldn't be able to take care of him and he would have to go to a nursing home. I told him that he would stay here until it was time for him to go "home, whether that was a week, a month or a year." It was at this time that I fully understood how frightened he was about going to a nursing home.

The Friday before Rick went into a deep coma, he had three distinct hallucinations.

1. I went to the store while he was sleeping. When I got back home a few minutes later, he was sitting up in the bed, something he hadn't done in a long time. The lights were on, and he had somehow gotten his wallet out of his nightstand. He calmly looked me in the eye and said with his booming baritone voice which had suddenly returned, "Who are these people?" I asked him to describe his visitors. He said that they were a Black man and woman. He wanted to know why they were there. I told him that they were there to escort him home. He said "Oh." I then asked him if he was afraid and he said "No." He told me, "Bea, you need to get my black pants, I have got to go." I quietly thought to myself… the end is near.

2. I went upstairs to make some phone calls and had given him a bell to ring if he needed me. Rick rang the bell. Immediately, I came downstairs and

Rick wanted to know who let that dog into the house. I asked him if the dog was Freckles, Phyllis and Don's dog who had died and Rick really loved. He told me "No." I then told him that the dog probably belonged to the man and woman and that it seemed like a nice dog and it was OK for him to stay. I asked him if the visitors were still here and he said "Yes." Funny thing, I wasn't afraid at all. I knew that I needed to do whatever I could to keep his altered sense of reality intact.

3. The bell rang again. I was talking to family members on the phone upstairs, but immediately I came back down stairs. He was up on his arms and told me that I needed to "clean up his house because it was a mess." This was WAYYYY out of character. Rick strongly disliked any form of housework. I told him that it wasn't messy (Ops... forgot the basic fact in dealing the dying you don't argue with them). He told me to forget it and that he would get up and clean it himself. Rick then started to get out of bed. I then told him that if he got out of bed, he would have to go to a nursing home because he couldn't afford to fall again. This "threat" was the only thing that he feared. I told him that I would clean up the house and he was not to worry. He then calmed down and closed his eyes. You don't have to be a rocket scientist to understand the "clean up his house" analogy. This was the last sentence he ever spoke to me.

The next day, while I was painting at Ruth's, Monique, who is both an in-home health specialist and my niece, was attending to Rick. I called to check on him, and she told me that she couldn't wake Uncle Rick. I immediately came home to find out what was happening.

Transition

Rick had slipped into a coma. The hospice nurse came out and told us that he didn't have much longer to live and asked if there was anyone who wanted to say goodbye to him. We were told that hearing is the last sense to leave. I immediately started making phone calls. Many of his relatives and friends called him and said goodbye to him.

Ruth and Larry K. came over to say goodbye to Rick. Women are very comfortable showing their emotions, while this is normally not a strong suit for most men. Larry came into Rick's sick room as he lay in a semi-comatose state and gently kissed him on the forehead. Larry said, *"Hey, Buddy, save a place at the table for me."* It was so deeply touching and even in his comatose state Rick grunted in acknowledgment of Larry's presence.

Rick would move his lips and try to respond, if there was conversation in the room. Whenever I would enter the room, he would become more animated and increased his movements. The nurse told me that his love for me was keeping him here even though he was trying to make his transition to another life. She told me to kiss him goodbye and to go upstairs and he would be gone in the morning.

Rick started his "death rattle." This sounds like a fish out of water and can be quite disconcerting to witness. I was told by hospice to turn him on his side and make him comfortable. Next, I was instructed to increase his pain medicine and keep him as comfortable as possible. My son, daughter-in-law, Debbie and Monique, were with me during this final phase. Rick's New England family and my daughter, Wendy, were in constant contact by phone. I kissed him goodbye and told him that I loved him, thanked him for loving me, my children, and our grandchildren. I then told him that it was OK for him to go and be with his Mother and Jesus. I then went upstairs with Debbie and went to sleep.

Later, I woke up at about 2:00 AM and went back downstairs. (I always had a problem following directions.) He was literally expiring. You have heard of the term, but literally he was taking short breaths as he was crossing over to the other side. I kissed him and told him that it will be all right, but to let me know when he leaves. Some may think that this is a bunch of "mumbo jumbo", and you are entitled to your opinion, but at 6:30 AM I suddenly woke up again and knew he was gone. Rick always gave me a little kiss when he left for work in the morning. I came downstairs and the Native American CD, *Canyon Trilogy* by R. Carlos Nakai, was still playing. Debbie was downstairs in the kitchen retrieving voice-mail messages. Rick was no longer breathing. His eyes and mouth were open and he had the face of an angel. I then removed the pillow that I used to prop him up towards the end—and it was still warm. I started to cry and tightly held on to this pillow until it no longer radiated his body heat. My biggest fear all along was that he would suffer horribly and end up all twisted and contorted when he died. He was quiet and so dignified as he made his transition. Observing his final moments became such a sacred and religious experience for all of us. When my time comes, I only pray that I can handle it with even a portion of his grace and dignity.

A benefit of having hospice as part of this process was that all I had to do was to contact them and they came over immediately to assist our family. Since his death was an expected death at home, it was not necessary for anyone to contact the Coroner's Office. Hospice contacted the funeral home and disposed of his prescription drugs.

Phone Tree Notification List

In preparing for his death and the associated chaos, I developed a Phone Tree Notification List. All I had to do was to call about four people and they put the telephone tree concept into play. Having this list greatly reduced my mounting stress level by allowing these friends to make the calls for me.

PHONE TREE NOTIFICATION

Responsible Person	Person To Call	Relationship	Phone Number	Comments
Bea Bailey	Denise Bailey	Step-Daughter		
	Richard Bailey	Step-Son		
	Linda Johnston	Sister-in-law		Linda will contact the other siblings.
	Wendy Allen, Rodney Ellison	Daughter, Son		
	Debbie, Ellouise, Diane Keating and Wendell Nance	Bea's Sisters and Brother		
Aubrey H.	He will contact the Church and other key friends.	Friend		
Joan A.	She will contact Bea's Friends			

Broadcast E-Mail

Since I had time to prepare prior to Rick's death, I created a draft version of a **broadcast e-mail** that informed people that he had passed. In this e-mail, I informed people of the date and time of his death. I also took the opportunity to thank them for their concern, but asked that they not call at this time as I was not able to respond to them. This e-mail cut down on the calls, but a few still came through.

My son, Champy, who has dealt with death in his capacity with the highway patrol, responded like the cavalry. In he came with a box of donuts. There apparently is some strange relationship between law enforcement officers and donuts. Champy then took total control of the situation and coordinated the transport of Rick's body to the funeral home. My son loved Rick so much and was honored to handle this difficult task.

Next, Champy contacted the medical supply people to come out and pick up the rented hospital equipment. When they stated that they couldn't pick up the equipment until that evening, he had Rick's friend, Aubrey, help him dismantle the sick room and take the equipment into the garage. Our neighbor, Cindy, directed him in rearranging the room. My girlfriend, Denise was there and had me go out onto the deck when the mortuary came for Rick's body. While they rearranged the living room, she took me for a walk and when I came back, there was no trace of a sick room and easy listening jazz was quietly playing.

> Rick's **obituary had been written in advance**. I had previously submitted a draft to the *Sacramento Bee* and was aware of the cost of the obituary. All I had to do was to insert the appropriate dates, details, and e-mail the paper this updated information. Their representative contacted me, obtained my credit card information, and the obituary was in the paper the next day.

Create a Calendar of Events with Phone Numbers

A key component in trying to juggle all of the balls that will be thrown everyone's way is having a **central calendar of events**. While this is not a party that you are planning, there are a lot of variables that have to be handled during this time. I created a calendar on my computer with key arrival times and phone numbers so that anyone could look at it and know what was what. Any standard calendar that is large enough to write on will work. I would suggest having some correction tape handy, if you opt to write in pen. Post it in an obvious place, like on the refrigerator, so everyone will have easy access as the final plans roll out.

My sister, Ellouise was in route and would be here in a couple of days. My friends were in constant contact with me and I did have my many lists to write. However, since I took care of Rick in our home for 18 months, I still found myself listening for his call. Once, I was in bed and was looking through a phone book. I then tossed it on the floor when I was done reading it. I gasped and thought, "Oh, no. I might wake Rick up downstairs." I had to then stop and realized that he wasn't down there. On other occasions, I would make myself something to eat and then stop and go to dish up some for Rick, but he wasn't there. You will be surprised how much you included your loved one into your daily activities.

Then the food starting arriving... My former boss from Xerox, Larry M., barbequed enough food for our entire complex. My Bible study group then went into action and before I knew it, my entire refrigerator and counters were overflowing. The amount of food that was brought was simply overwhelming. In retrospect, I would suggest that people try to coordinate their efforts. Perhaps, a **gift certificate** to a store near the bereaved one's home would be a better option. When a grocery need came up, the certificate could be used. If not, you may have food in your house that might ultimately spoil.

A friend and former boss of mine from Xerox, Frank L., contacted me and said that he wanted to do something special. He then arranged for 10 dozen long stem red roses to be delivered to the church for Rick's memorial service. Denise met the florist at the church and created one-of-a-kind bouquets for the service and the repast. What a wonderful gesture of friendship. I was also able to then give a single red rose to those in attendance who had been particularly kind to us. Linda also took a large bouquet home with her to New England.

DEATH OF A LOVED ONE
ACTION ITEMS

Done (X)	Item	Required Action	Status	Comments

NUT BOX

Done (X)	Item	Status
	Key contact phone list for family members	
	Social Security cards	
	Marriage license	
	Medical personnel contact numbers.	
	Safety deposit keys	
	Extra Set of house keys	
	Obituary	
	Extra set of car keys	
	Insurance Policies	
	Mock-up of funeral program	
	Loved one's wallet	
	Birth certificate, yours and your spouse's, if you are married.	
	Loved one's car keys	
	Security badge and or keys from work, if appropriate	

PHONE TREE NOTIFICATION

Responsible Person	Person To Call Item	Relationship	Phone Number	Comments

There Was a Bit of Humor
Surrounding Rick's Death

Are you depressed enough yet? I thought so, so here are some really funny things that happened surrounding the death of my father and Rick's dying experience. Life can be and is funny, and Rick and I laughed almost up to the very end. Some of these funny times are what I remember about my father's and Rick's death. They have sustained me and brought a smile to my face whenever I think about this entire experience.

o   When my father, who was a minister, was dying in 1983, I had read the book *Life After Death*, by Elisabeth Kübler-Ross. Upon my arrival at his bedside, he was saying that the "holy man" was coming. In this book, Kübler-Ross talks about a Christ-like figure that many people saw before they died. Well, being the little professor that I am, I thought that it would be a great idea to ask him if he was on this side or the other and get some firsthand insight into life after death. I asked Daddy if he was on this side or the other side? He looked up at me, and said, "Hell no!" What are you talking about? You are the damnest child I ever had!" Clearly, he was not on the other side and was still very much a part of this world.

o   When Rick was sleeping a lot, he was fairly non-communicative and his friends understood. One day I came in to check on him, and he was alert, full of fun and really hungry. I said, "Lazarus, you are back!" We both started laughing and I gave him a big fat kiss.

- We had long-term health care insurance and were fortunate enough to have in-home care eight hours a day. When one of the health care people, initially assigned to our case, asked if Rick had any "decubitus." I immediately went into a panic mode. Lord knows I had tried to think of everything that he would need to be comfortable at home. I told her that he didn't, but did she know where I could get some for him, I would go and purchase it. She looked at me like I had lost my mind. "Decubitus" is the medical term for bed sores, and thank goodness, he didn't have any.

- Rick was looped up on morphine for a while. When I asked him if he was in La La Land, he said that he was definitely in La La Land. I asked him what it looked like. He said that La La Land was pretty and had lots of colorful "La Las" lying around.

- Initially Rick had to wear a brace to protect his spine after his back surgery. When my grandson, Christopher, came to town to visit, we took him to Papa's bedside. We showed him his brace. Later that night, while I was reading to him, Christopher quietly told me that Papa was sick, but he did look a lot like Superman!

- When Rick had just died, Denise and Aubrey immediately came over to support me. While we were waiting for the mortuary staff and drinking tea, Denise impishly pointed to two of my fabric chairs and said, "Rick really wanted me to have those chairs... and the silk plant in the hallway and your new silver retro fan... ah seriously." We all burst into laughter because it was so off the wall and so funny. What a tension breaker! I still laugh when I think of this comment.

o I had planned to spend the night of Rick's death at our home because I knew that I was a big girl and would be OK, *particularly with all of the lights on*. Champy and Nokie insisted that I spend the night with them, which in retrospect was a good idea. I slept with my grandson, Isaac, that night. When we were nestled in bed talking, he showed me his white teddy bear with gold wings and a halo. He said that this was his "Papa" bear and that Papa had died, was now an angel and in heaven. I told him that that was true. Isaac then looked up at me and said, "Mimi, you know, you are 'kinda' old and you are going to die, too!" I tried not to burst out laughing and told him that I would eat right, exercise, and go to the doctor to make sure that this didn't happen soon. He looked up at me with that "good-luck-with-that" smile, and said, "OK… but it's gonna happen." Out of the mouths of babes…Whew!!!

Eventually, I did have to go home. Laughter or not, I suddenly found myself dealing with a gigantic vacuum and did not know what to do. I strongly leaned on my lists and found myself making lists of my lists and then listing them on other lists. I was headed for some emotional trouble and could feel a mounting scream growing inside of me.

Rick's Final Services

Viewing Rick's Body

Morgan and Jones Mortuary had arranged for us to view Rick's body prior to the general viewing. If you opt to have a public viewing, you will then understand why the mortuary first has a private viewing for the family members. I had seen Rick right after he had died so I knew what he would look like. My son had told me that I needed to prepare myself for the fact that it had been a week since he died and he probably wouldn't look good. When I arrived at the viewing, my sister Debbie and my son were waiting. When I entered with my daughter and Ellouise and saw Rick lying in his casket, sounds came out of me that were both foreign and frightening to everyone in the room. They scared both of my children and me, too. Rick looked so healthy and handsome. If you didn't look at his shriveled body from the neck down, he looked like he was just sleeping with the sweetest smile on his face. *I wanted to scream at him and tell him to get up out of that coffin because he was now scaring everyone because they thought that he was dead!* In many situations, your loved one might not look like themselves due to the nature of their death and associated trauma. However for me, the gift that Morgan and Jones gave me was that my last view of Rick was a view of a man who looked like the handsome man that I had married 13 years before. It was so wonderful and so equally sad.

My children were very supportive of me and were very upset over Rick's death. My son, Champy, who sees death on a regular basis in his line of work, as a law enforcement officer, was more upset than he had anticipated. My daughter couldn't stop crying. I told both of them that Rick was more than a step-father; he was a "bonus" dad. A "bonus dad" is a dad without all the parent-child drama that normally comes in a family, or at least in my family. Rick loved me, my children and our grandchildren unconditionally. We will never be the same without him.

Rick's sister, Linda ("Red Hawk Woman") and her husband, Jim, came out from Connecticut to represent the New England family. It was gut-wrenching to see her standing and crying at her big brother's coffin. They all are such a close family and Rick was the first of the six siblings to die. Sadly, in less than a year and a half, this family lost two additional siblings.

During this family viewing, my son raided my wallet and took out pictures I had of his children and Wendy's son and gently placed them on the inside lid of Rick's coffin. He also left a souvenir from the California Highway Patrol to honor Rick out of respect for how Rick supported him during his time as a cadet at the academy. Debbie, being the ever present cut-up that she is, slipped a miniature version of a slot machine into the coffin just under the ruffles by his hands. Rick and Debbie were good gambling buddies. She said that when she went to purchase the slot machine, the store owner said that it had a buzzer that might shock the recipient of the gift. Debbie calmly stated that this would not be a problem. This is a good time to restate that if you have young children or other adults who have special items that they want to bury with the love one, you should try to gather these objects in advance and have them ready prior to the funeral. We didn't do this, but I wished that we had.

Many of Rick's work friends, as well as our church members, came to view his body. I stayed for the entire time and greeted and thanked everyone. Depending on your own emotional state, you might want to opt for less time. I lived about 20 miles away and it would have been too much of a production to see him, go home, and then drive back down through rush hour traffic for visitation, so I opted to stay.

Then a most curious thing happened. A woman from his previous job came to view the Rick's body. I went and spoke to her and introduced myself thanked her for coming. She rolled her eyes and tersely said that she KNEW who I was; I was the former Xerox representative for their company. I thought, "Now that was strange." Later, I put two and two together and remembered that she was in hot pursuit of Rick when I started dating him 14 years earlier. He worked at a company where I had just sold a series of Xerox copiers. I couldn't help but laugh to myself later on and think, *"Goodness gracious, woman, the man married me and now is dead...let it go ... just let it go!"*

 It was not until Rick's death that I fully understood the depth of the love that Nokie, my daughter-in-law had for Rick. During his memorial service, she said in a broken voice that if she told Rick that she wanted to be an astronaut, he would simple say, "Great, Baby, just get some books and read up on it and you can do it!" Nokie is part Vietnamese and Chinese and came at the end of the public viewing. She had a beautiful yellow chrysanthemum plant with her. Nokie then performed a

Vietnamese reverence ceremony. She sobbed uncontrollably as she knelt on the floor and bowed three times in reverence towards "Papa's" casket. Next, she turned and bowed three times towards me. She then asked Ellouise, Wendy, and me to follow her actions. We then took a single yellow blossom and took the petals off of it. The loose petals were then sprinkled over his hands so that he would be able to find us in the afterlife. Tears... Wails... you have no idea of the depth of anguish and flood of emotions that were contained within the walls of that room during this ceremony

Rick's Memorial Service

Rick's memorial service was a week after his death. The week immediately following his death was a blur. Rick had stated that he didn't want his body at the church lying in state for his grandchildren to see. The service was very uplifting with many friends and co-workers attending. All of his favorite songs were sung.

Native American Flute was played by Ellen RH, while his sister, Linda, "Red Hawk Woman", read a poem wearing her full Native American regalia. The poem was entitled, "The Sundance Prayer." Linda started out by saying, "Hanta Yo (clear the way). The poem stated that Rick's spirit goes forth and makes the light. He was the center of all things and everything flowed from him. He would live forever. He was "Grey Wolf" and he was at peace. She then said, "Acqua Ne" which means "Go (Walk) in Peace My Brother." Ah, Ho or Amen. This was very moving experience to all in attendance.

Our granddaughter, Sascha Ellison, was unable to attend the services, but was considerate enough to send an e-mail expressing her condolences to be read during the service. In her e-mail, Sascha wrote:

> *I still can't believe it's true. I will still expect to see you on my next visit down there. You were the nicest, most loving down to earth person I know and I hate saying you "were" because I don't want to face the fact of you no longer being here. So I won't. As far as I am concerned, you are still here but just in a different place.*
>
> *I have never experienced death like this before. Even though we had a warning, nothing could have prepared me for it. The pain that I felt was not like any other. A pain if I never feel again would be too soon. Grandpa Rick, I love you so much.*
>
> *Words could never explain what you meant to me. You were the first person to take me on a boat ride and the first person to take me fishing. Events I will never forget. Even now, I have not come to terms with your leaving. You are no longer here, but you will forever stay in my HEART. FOREVER.*

Sending an e-mail to be read at the service is an excellent vehicle for someone who is unable to attend the service, but still wants to make a statement regarding their feelings for a loved one.

Another touching moment came when Bruno, Rick's friend, read a poem. Bruno, the Gentle Giant that he was, asked me if it was OK to read a poem about war and death. Rick and Bruno were "room dogs" when they were in the Air Force and had remained fast friends. The poem is entitled, "The Beach". It is written by Oscar Brown Jr., and compares death to soldiers storming a beach. This was so apropos because Rick loved anything to do with World War II. The poem basically states, in part, "Not one will manage to survive. Nobody leaves this beach alive." Everyone in attendance was touched by this wonderful poem. Bruno handed me a copy of the poem and it was signed, "From one soldier to another, Nate Boyce." With Rick's tremendous pride of his 30-year military service, I know he loved this poem read by this battle scarred veteran. Ironically, Bruno followed Rick in death a few months later.

Another traditional poem which is often read at funerals was also part of Rick's service. It is such a haunting yet comforting poem. It is a follows:

If Tomorrow Starts Without Me

When tomorrow starts without me and I'm not there to see.

If the sun should rise and find your eyes, all filled with tears for me.

I wish so much you wouldn't cry, the way you did today,

While thinking of the many things we didn't get to say.

I know how much you love me, as much as I love you.

And each time that you think of me, I know you'll miss me, too.

But when tomorrow starts without me, please try to understand,

That an angel came and called my name, and took me by the hand.

And said my place was ready, in Heaven far above,

And that I'd have to leave behind, all those I dearly love.

But as I turned to walk away, a tear fell from my eye.

For all life, I'd always thought, I didn't want to die.

I had so much to live for, so much yet to do.

It seemed almost impossible, that I was leaving you.

So when tomorrow starts without me, don't think we're far apart.

For every time you think of me, I'm right here, in your heart.

—Author Unknown

I had arranged for doves to be released at the end of the service. Rick loved aviation so much that I thought that doves taking off would look like a bunch of little white planes soaring overhead. The dove handler wanted a key family member to release the lead dove. Punkin stated that he wanted to do it. He did a great job and the ceremony was beautiful. Of course,

Isaac wanted his own lead bird and Christopher was mad at Punkin because he had let go of the bird!   As the birds were released, we all shouted "acqua ne", a Native American term which means, "Go (Walk) in Peace My Brother."

Don Bailey of Pulsar Productions created a DVD of the service that I sent to family members back east who were unable to attend. It ended with the song that stated that the person was going up to heaven to be with Jesus and was sung by Brenda H., a close personal friend of ours. Don videotaped the doves circling higher and higher to coincide with the lyrics. The DVD then faded into a picture of Rick smiling on top of the clouds. It was an extremely moving and comforting DVD. You might want to consider this DVD option, too, for friends or relatives, who for a variety of reasons are not able to attend the service.

We then had a barbeque at Champ and Nokie's house and a good time was had by all. Just before leaving the barbeque, Ruth came up to me. She had a small gift box in her hand and a card. She said that it was for me and that I should open it when I got home in private. I was instructed to open the box first and then read the card. When I did get home, I did exactly as instructed. Inside the box was a beautiful heavy braided silver bracelet. I thought "what on earth?" I then read the card which was in Ruth's handwriting. It said: "Bea- Shortly before he passed, and in words that were barely audible, Rick asked us to find you a silver bracelet to replace one that was lost. We were privileged to be his couriers. Ruth and Larry". When I initially opened up the card, I immediately read Ruth's message, which was written upside down on the opposite cover. It wasn't until months later, during my birthday, when I read the other side that said "For Bea – From your grateful and adoring husband. Rick." All this time, I knew that he was absorbed in crossing over into another dimension, yet he made a point to think of me while he was dying and wanted to express his love to me even after he was gone. He had to have made this arrangement during one of their visits with Rick and I was out of the room for just a brief moment. I can't begin to tell you how happy and sad these touching acts made me feel.

On an upbeat note, the next day, I took all family members who were available out to Thunder Valley, the Indian Casino not far from our home. As stated before, Rick was an avid gambler and spent many an afternoon at Thunder Valley. Everyone enjoyed the seafood buffet and those who wanted to gamble… did so. We had a ball. I felt confident that he was there with us and cruising by his favorite quarter machine.

Rick's Burial Service

Prior to the burial, I had to stop by the mortuary and handle some more paperwork and get the directions for the burial. I took all of the greeting cards Rick has received, which numbered in the hundreds, as well as an 11 x 17 professional photograph of me in my wedding dress. He loved this photo so much and it hung on his side of the bedroom. I thought that it was only fitting that he be buried with this photo and the greeting cards. Ellouise was with me and asked if I wanted her to come inside with me because it might be upsetting. Oh, please, what do I look like, a baby? Once again, she was right. It was eerie and indeed upsetting being in a building and know that your spouse is somewhere in the building lying dead in a box.

OK, he had died two weeks ago. We had the memorial service last week, and now came the easy part, the burial, right?

 When you have a burial at a national cemetery, you have to coordinate the burial with available space and previously scheduled services. My sister Ellouise had gone back to Iowa, and, Linda and Jim had gone back to Connecticut. I was busy donating Rick's clothes and effects, and handling death-related paperwork. The mortuary had arranged for everything. I just needed to drive

down, participate in a brief ceremony and that was it. I knew that this would be a piece of cake. Right? ...wrong! With Ruth, Denise and Aubrey by my side, we were off to the San Joaquin Valley National Cemetery in Gustine, California. Aubrey had told Rick that he would be with him until the very end and he was. It was a two-hour trip and we played the CD *Canyon Trilogy* during the trip. This was the CD that Ruth gave me and it played non-stop during the final three days of Rick's life. I never played this CD again.

As I got out of the car and went in to fill out the paperwork, my buddy Ruth was by my side. Out of nowhere, the tears began to fall. I could barely see where I was walking. When I got back outside and stood in my assigned place, as his widow, I walked behind his coffin in a flood of tears. Just to think that he was *IN* that box was just breaking my heart.

The ceremony was beautiful, but so sad. The honor guard thanked me for Rick's service to our country. They restated how the colors of the flag corresponded to the red, white, and blue of his valor and bravery. Inside I was screaming for them to stop! They were slowly killing me with these emotional and patriotic sentiments. I saved each shell casing from his 21-gun salute and gave the shell casings to his siblings, son, grandchildren and close friends. The cemetery has a lake and I like to visualize Rick doing some heavenly fishing in that spot. His tombstone reads: "A Man Who Loved Both His Family & Country."

If Rick could have said anything to us, he perhaps would have said this poem:

I Did Not Die

Do not stand at my grave and weep.
I am not there; I do not sleep.

I am a thousand winds that blow.
I am the diamond glints on snow.
I am the sunlight on ripened grain.
I am the gentle autumn's rain.

When you wake up to morning's hush
I am the swift uplifting rush
Of quiet birds in circled flight.
I am the soft stars that shine at night.

Do not stand at my grave and cry.
I am not there. I did not die.

Anonymous

The death, memorial, and burial services were now done. The healing must now begin, but I knew then it wouldn't be overnight. What an understatement that turned out to be.

Financial Logistics and Required Actions

There are some important actions that you need to take place, as soon as is possible.

Death Certificates

First of all, you will need certified copies of the death certificate from your county Department of Health and Human Services. The mortuary that handled Rick's arrangements handled this detail for me. It took approximately two weeks for me to receive my copies. The time period will vary based upon workload in that department. There is little that you can do in finalizing any financial or legal matters after the death without a certified death certificate. However, you can make some initial calls regarding these matters to get the ball rolling. Your file may be opened up and preliminary steps taken as your case is set up pending the arrival of the actual the death certificate.

The cost for the death certificates at the time was $10 each. I could think of about 12 separate instances in which I needed certificates and consequently ordered 12 certified copies. Later, I discovered that I really didn't need that many certified copies. Most institutions require only a **copy** of certified death certificate and not the original. I really only needed about five. However, having a few extra copies on hand would cover any unforeseen future situation.

 Whenever I submitted information to any institution, I always wrote a cover letter with appropriate references to provide a paper trail in the event that something would go awry. I would strongly suggest that you do this and create individual file folders and place all correspondence in chronological order. Write down the key numbers inside the folders and in your spiral binders that you have been keeping up to date. This may seem like a bit much, but if you do this type of record keeping, you will thank me later.

The following situations required a death certificate:

Social Security Benefits

If you are over the age of 60, you may be eligible for your spouse's social security benefits. I contacted the local Social Security Field Office after Rick's death. While they required a certified death certificate, they interviewed me over the phone and obtained all of the necessary information to open my case. To finalize it, I made an appointment with the representative (I had gotten their name and phone number). When I met with them, they made a copy of the certified death certificate for their records and I started receiving my benefits the very next month. You can obtain a lot of pertinent information on the Social Security website.

A couple of pointers:

1) You should also set aside the estimated monthly benefit amount you anticipate to receive on hand in a separate savings account. This will cover you in the event that you might encounter a bureaucratic snag or two which might result in delayed payments.

2) Also, if there was a prior marriage, you will be asked questions about that as well. It helps to have the prior marriage's marriage license and divorce papers or at least the information on hand. I was told by the Social Security Administration representative that providing them with information on this prior union will not impact the amount of your eligible benefits.

Car Insurance

Believe it or not, you cannot make any changes to your car insurance policy unless you provide a copy of the death certificate. Think about it... without this legal requirement, if you were angry at your spouse or friend, you could just call up the insurance company and have them dropped from the policy. It is a nice layer of protection for all concerned, don't you think?

Life Insurance

You can investigate your life insurance benefits prior to the death of your loved one to find out more about the policy. There are different requirements to file a claim depending on the institution that is providing the coverage. Regardless of the requirements, a certified death certificate is definitely required here. Don't forget to get the name and direct dial number of the representative that you have contacted so that you do not end up in some voice-mail loop that is maddening.

Investments

Talk to your financial planner and/or banker to inform them of the death and you will be walked through the proper procedures to redistribute or rename these investments.

Medical Coverage

If you are covered by your spouse's medical benefits, there might be an overlapping or waiting period regarding your own medical coverage. Check with the appropriate human resources or Medicare/Aid personnel to find out how you are impacted in this regard. Try to find out this information in advance. If you have to change carriers or obtain your own coverage, you will have some time to find out what you need in advance so that there is no lapse in your benefits or coverage.

Please check and double-check any change requests you make during this first year. Although I had submitted a copy of the death certificate to stop Rick's medical coverage through my former employer, the administrative unit handling this matter did not act upon this request. I didn't pay attention to this matter until I received my annual medical enrollment document. When I reviewed it, I noted that Rick's name was active. After I had contacted them again and told them that he had passed, they corrected my records. A week later, I opened up my mail and was presented with a bill for almost $1,300. This bill was issued to cover the repayment of Medicare premiums that had been incorrectly credited towards my retirement allowance for health coverage during the past year. While I was furious because I had done what I needed to do on my end, the bill was still a valid bill and had to be paid. Even though you may submit the proper paperwork to stop dual coverage, it is incumbent upon you to double-check your pay stubs and related documents to make sure that your change requests have been implemented.

Updating Living Trust or Will

Once you receive your copy of the death certificate, you need to contact your attorney or whoever prepared your documents and make updated changes to the documents to reflect your current status. They will ask for a copy of the death certificate and will help you with the next step. Obtaining this information in advance will allow you to know what to do when the time comes.

By attending to these financial details, you are not being ghoulish or insensitive, but are getting ahead of the avalanche of paperwork required to settle an estate. There may be a time lag involved in all of the areas listed, so the sooner you contact these organizations, the sooner this area will be properly addressed. Again, even with this preparation, you might forget a thing or two, but you WILL have the lion's share of this information at your fingertips and be able to set specific elements in motion.

FINANCIAL LOGISTICS AND REQUIRED ACTIONS CHECKLIST

ACTION ITEMS

Done (X)	Item	Required Action	Status	Comments

Grief, "Closure" and Moving On

"Protect me, dear Lord, My boat is so small, And your sea is so big."
—*Greasley Church Website*

"Everyone can master grief, but he that has it."
—*Much Ado About Nothing*

You are on your own here because this topic is such an individual journey… but, I will try to help you out a bit.

Rick Actually Died and Will NEVER Come Back to Me

All the books and all the thoughts I had regarding how I was going to handle this area had to be tossed out the window. (Well, that is a tad bit of an exaggeration) How can you wrap your head around the concept that someone who you loved was an integral part of your life and now is gone? I knew that Rick was terminally ill and would die, but did that really mean I would not see him again? In retrospect, I think I was fairly convinced that after Rick died he would then move to a special colony in Lodi, California or in Cleveland, Ohio. I could just stop in, have week-end visitations, drink a couple of cups of tea with him, and catch up on things. After about nine months, I slowly began to understand that when you die, you do actually go away *forever*. I understood all of this in my head, but not my heart.

When something large is moved out of a room, there is a perceptible echo due to the resulting emptiness. I found that not only did our home echo, but my life now began to echo. This grief is a deep ache and a feeling of emptiness that nothing can fill. It is a quiet, non-stop, nightmare that you think you are going to wake up from... but you don't.

I started to shop...and, actually, I never stopped... but honestly, how many more cute tops can you buy? I had donated or given away the majority of Rick's clothes and now found all the closets filled with *my* clothes. More clothes...Now, remember, I am retired; shouldn't I need fewer clothes and not an additional closet full of new ones? This was becoming more than "retail therapy." And let's talk about shopping at Costco. Old habits are hard to die... but did I really need 48 rolls of toilet paper for one single adult? I needed some shopping intervention right now! *Dat Gum It!...* *Where is Ruth?*

 A hard part of the grieving process is that people don't know what to say to you. Heck, I don't know what to say to me! Every time that I went anywhere... a memory of him was there or someone was there to mention how much they missed him and to ask how I was doing. I had a Christian friend who told me that I needed to stop all of that grieving, and not to worry because I will see him again when I get to Heaven. All I wanted to do was to punch out her lights. I know that I will see him in Heaven, but that did not offer me any comfort at this stage of my grief process and when I am lying in a cold bed at night.

"I Am So Sorry to Hear About Your Loss"

What do you say and what do you do when someone has lost a loved one? People will mumble and stumble when they see you because of their own level of discomfort. They want the bereaved to snap out it to ease their own pain and uneasiness. They try to help you find something positive in your suffering. The truth of the matter is that it takes time to traverse through your grief. Do not, I repeat, do not allow anyone to push you prematurely through this process.

I would like to offer you some suggestions on how I was helped or could have been helped during my grieving.

1. When someone has lost a loved one, be direct. Look them in the eye and simply tell them, "I am sorry to hear about _____'s death. He/she was a wonderful person and will be missed."

2. Ask them how they are actually feeling. Sometimes people dance around this because they are afraid that they will be unable to answer the second level questions that might follow when you do in fact tell them how you are feeling.

3. Don't say that you can empathize with them. Unless YOU personally have lost a similar loved one under similar circumstances, you don't know how they feel. You can sympathize with them, but true empathy only comes when you have walked in similar shoes. Recently, my brother-in-law lost two brothers within 90 days. When I attended the funeral of the second brother, his mother was sitting in the lobby waiting for the services to start. She was in a state of shock. I just came up to her, kissed her on the cheek, and told her that I loved her and didn't know what to say. It was not the time to for some empty platitudes. Nothing else could be said because I couldn't imagine the level of pain that she was going through, I just wanted her to know that I cared. In fact, I pray that I will never have to empathize with her.

4. NEVER give advice about how someone should get through the loss. On more than one occasion, I was told that "Rick wouldn't want me to be so sad and that I needed to get on with my life." Outside, I gave a weak smile, nodded and said, "Thank you." Inside, I was screaming "Oh, Shut up and get away from me!" Be open to the mourner's individual needs and to the possibility that these needs will change day by day.

5. I often use laughter to lessen the tension in a situation and a person who is grieving might appreciate this effort. However, you have to know your audience before your opt to don a party hat and a funny nose. It might go over like a lead balloon. If you want to say something uplifting, then tell them a funny story or anecdote about your loved one or how they have had a positive impact on your life. This gesture may bring a smile to their face.

 We could take a page out of the animal kingdom in trying to find out how to console a person who has suffered a loss. Elephants form a circle around the bereaved and loop their trunks together in support. The Musk Oxen form a circle around the wounded animal to form a barrier against any possible predator. Those experiencing a loss will need you support much more AFTER the death of your loved one than during the initial stages.

My grieving was a lot like pulling a band aid off a sore time and time again. How can I then heal? When I went to church two weeks after Rick had died, a friend came up to me and said that he had been thinking about Rick on the way to church and wanted to know how the Brother was doing. I took a deep breath and told him that he had died two weeks earlier. He felt just awful and I then found myself consoling him in his grief. My church is large and this happened on four separate occasions.

The fact of the matter is that grieving can only be handled one day at a time and sometimes one hour at a time. It sounds like such a cliché and in so many ways it is, but it is so true. The adage says, *Time heals all wounds*, but the scars and the lingering pains will always be there to some degree.

The key is to get past the first year. "Everyone" says that you shouldn't make any changes during the first year if possible and this is true. It will take you at least that long just to try to balance your life. If you work, then going back to work might help to bring some form and process to your life. I was retired and didn't have to work and could do what I wanted to do… except I didn't know what to do. I had spent so much time as a hard-charging corporate woman and then as a two-year caregiver that now having total freedom was daunting to me. I was in a mental free-fall and it was surprisingly scary and unnerving.

Loss of Identity

But how? How the devil could I go on as *Mrs. Rick Bailey*, when there was no longer a *Mr. Rick Bailey*? The sadness and sense of loss was overwhelming at times. I had lost not only a friend and confidant, but a sense of my identity and my rudder. I didn't feel married anymore, but I certainly didn't feel single. Whenever I would travel to visit my daughter in Los Angeles, after putting my suitcases down, I would always head to the phone to let Rick know that I had arrived safely. I then had to stop and realize that he wasn't at home waiting for my call. When I saw a great historical documentary or received the latest edition of the *Smithsonian* on Egypt, I would take it out of the mailbox and head into the house to share it with him… but he wasn't there.

My loss was even sharper because I had cared for him in our home for almost 18 months and he had passed away there. After Rick died, I had time, lots of time on my hands and was conscious of not filling up my schedule with too much because I knew that I had to grieve and mend. I had to get back to a normal schedule and I knew that, but what exactly was a *normal* schedule? I have often said that when I die and meet him, I will give him a smack for leaving such a big hole in my heart and then a gigantic hug!

The year after his death, his tribe held a Crossing Over Ceremony in Connecticut. It was the last official act that I had to perform as his wife. I was looking forward to visiting both his family and my sister and her family. When I changed planes in Chicago, I had to go the Concourse "C". This was no big deal, because we had taken this trip many times. As I walked towards the Concourse, I was overwhelmed by an oppressive sadness to the extent I had to stop and catch my breath. Rick was not there with me as he had been on so many other occasions. I felt so alone and out of sorts and this reaction was totally unexpected. During your season of grief, you too will have many similar experiences as you are attempting to retool your life.

During the actual ceremony, Jerry, my brother-in-law, decided to participate in a ceremonial dance that was reserved to honor veterans who had served our country. This action was so out of character for Jerry who is extremely shy and reserved. He walked past me and told me that he had to do this to say goodbye to Rick and to honor his memory. Once again I was reduced to tears as I observed him sadly performing this sacred dance in honor of his buddy, Rick.

Some days were better than others, but this time period was a tremendous struggle for me. So many people felt that I was "OK" because, after all I was *Beatrice Bailey, Mighty Warrior Princess*, right? Wrong. I fought to be aware of my emotions and not to fool myself. Well, my body told me what was happening. Stress … pure latent stress, filtering through my body. During this process I lost almost 18 pounds. Rick really liked for me to wear my hair long and in view of the fact that that was one of the few things he asked me to do, I humored him and let it grow out. Well, he must have really liked it, because when he died about eight inches of my hair fell out and he must have decided to take it with him! You can't be on deck for 18 months with all of your senses in high gear without having it take a physical toll on your body.

Quiet as it was kept; I came painfully close to a nervous breakdown and was fighting tooth and nail not to fall into a deep emotional abyss. I was like a turtle with its shell ripped off. Even a slight brush with a small leaf would send me into an emotional tailspin. While vacation in Greece, I continued to have one panic attack after another. This intensified after I thought that I had lost my passport. I had left it on the bus and the guide was able to retrieve it. While they were retrieving my passport, I kept kicking myself and screaming inside, *"Damn it, Rick, if you had been with me this wouldn't have happened!"* Rick was so good about handling all of our traveling papers during our many trips and making the currency conversions. As I tried to sleep on the ship, I was hit with one panic attack after another and it was oppressive. My friend, Diana, was very supportive, but there was little she could do to help me out of this emotional spiral. This is when my strong religious belief went into overdrive. Many of the places we visited in Greece and Turkey are discussed in the Bible. One night as I lay in a sweat trying to catch my breath, I remembered the passage in the Bible when the tempest was raging and Jesus, on waters similar to these, simply said, "Peace be still" (Luke Chapter 8). If he could calm these raging waters, Jesus was able to calm the raging waters of my personal tempest. After this, my panic attacks did go completely away, but I definitely had fewer attacks.

But Rick was everywhere I went. When I went to the Parthenon, the Beehive Tomb, the ruins of Ephesus and the Temple of Delphi, all I could think about was how much a history buff like Rick would have loved this trip. It was Rick, Rick and then more Rick throughout the trip.

If you feel that you are overwhelmed and confused, relax; it is a natural feeling. This is also a good time to have a full check-up with your medical doctor and psychologist. Even with my lists and charts and action plans, on many days I just found myself walking around in circles, forgetting why I came into a room, what I was supposed to be doing at that very minute, let alone that day. Honestly —how many episodes of *Law and Order* (All of them) and *CSI* (All of them) can one person watch on TV? For someone who has "always" been on top of things, I was lost. I innocently thought that once Rick had died and I had taken care of "closure" details, my life would get back to normal. Much to my surprise, I discovered that after his death the real work began. Ruth was very aware of my mental state. On more than one occasion, I caught her eyeballing me trying to determine my exact melt-down point.

During the year after Rick died, I had several distinct dreams or visitations from him. They were as follows:

- About a month after he died, I felt him sitting on the chaise lounge in our bedroom smiling at me as I knelt down to pray.

- I had a vivid dream about him in which he looked great, was happy and took me by the shoulders and told me that he was so proud of how I had been handling myself, but it was time for me to get on with my life.

- Once I thought that I had set both my cell phone alarm and my regular alarm clocks to make sure that I got up early and ate before I went to the gym. I had been losing an alarming amount of weight and needed to eat before I worked out. At 7:15 AM, I woke up because someone was shaking me. Rick had a distinct way of waking me. I looked around and there was no Rick. I then realized that I had NOT set either alarm clock … mmm?

- In February 2006, I went with Diana to Toluca, Mexico for a week's spa vacation. It was relaxing, but I was still extremely stressed at this time.

Spring 2007 – Bea having "fun" in Mexico

The next month I had a dream that I was back in Toluca and that Rick was waiting for me in a large hacienda. I ran down to the hacienda and went upstairs. He was lying in bed under a sheet in a bedroom that looked just like ours. I was really happy and got out of my clothes to slip into bed to snuggle with him. However, the second that I got into bed, he popped up fully dressed and tossed some clothing onto the chaise lounge. He said that there is no laundry facility where he was and I needed to get these things cleaned. Then he simply disappeared.

☐ Punkin told me that he had a dream about his Papa playing poker with God and Jesus. It was a nice to hear that he, too, was mending and having a pleasant dream about Rick.

Believe what you want, I know what I experienced. After the last dream, I have seldom felt his presence. I have been told that the spirit of your loved one hangs around until you no longer have a need for that level of comfort. I still talk to him from time to time, but the deep sadness is not there. I miss him something awful, but am no longer as sad. However, I still marvel that someone can be in your life for many years, then actually die and go away. It is still hard for me to fully understand this concept.

Closure and moving on is an individual journey. In some areas you will be able to "close" pretty quickly, but others will unfold in their own time. I decided to take off my **wedding ring** after Rick had been gone for two months, found that I wasn't ready and had to continue wearing it. I didn't wear it to Greece in the fall of 2006 and planned not to put it back on when I returned, but again, that proved to be too difficult. I made a mental decision that I would take off my wedding ring in January 2007, seven months after his death. January came and went and I was still wearing the ring. Taking it off would not speed up the grieving process any faster. I knew I would take it off one day, but I did not know when. Just because I said it was time, my heart and emotions said something else. Don't rush yourself in any area and don't hesitate to get some psychological and spiritual counseling.

My Mourning Journey

There are many books and articles written on the various steps and stages of mourning. You will find them on the Internet or at your local bookstores. They are written to address the various stages of grieving. There are many approaches to handling this subject and you will find many options.

Children's reaction to a death, however, requires specific treatment. After Rick's death, a lot of emphasis was placed upon how Punkin would handle the loss of his Papa. However, Nokie, my daughter-in-law, told me that one afternoon Isaac came downstairs. He was wailing at the top of his lungs and said that he missed his Papa and that he would never see him again. This was a delayed reaction and just ripped out our hearts. I am not an expert in dealing with this type of loss and would strongly suggest that you address this issue professionally, if this is your situation. If left untreated, symptoms may manifest themselves in a myriad of ways. This matter can be further researched on the Internet or at your local library. By doing this, you will be prepared to ask informed questions of your mental health professional when you are starting to address this situation.

If you are dealing with the death of a child, I don't even know where to begin. Someone once told me that when you decide to have a child, you are deciding to have your heart walk outside of your body forever. I don't even want to attempt to deal with this subject; because I thank the Lord I have no experience in this area.

You didn't misplace your purse, break a nail or lose a pet. You lost an integral part of your life. These variables associated with how you deal with this loss will be different when you are dealing with the death of a friend or someone who is not a spouse. While it is not the end of the world, it is the end of your world as you know it and your life will not be the same again. It will be different, but not the same.

My experience with handling my grief and mourning was as follows:

1) **Rick Died and Is Not On an Extended Vacation**

This concept is something that is really hard to comprehend. Unless you have experienced this, you can't begin to understand it. Your loved one is gone and it is impossible for you to ever see him or her again. As I stated earlier, I had to come to terms that Rick was not at some commune for the dearly departed that I could visit from time to time. Denying this fact only prolongs the entire grief process. This acceptance is not an overnight process, but a necessary one.

2) **Emotional Missiles:**

Those That You Launch and Those That Are Hurled At You

During this time, you will be extremely sensitive. EVERYTHING that normally did not bother you just might and will bother you. In dealing with my pain, I made lists.

Right after Rick's funeral, my sister Ellouise was still visiting me. As we sat in my guest bedroom, she watched me prepare my 10 pages of list of things to do. She quietly told me that I would run out of things to do and that the grieving process would have to start. I listened to her and then bit her head off and told her that lists is what I do and I will get to my grieving in MY OWN time. Sorry… Ellouise.

Your emotions will be all over the map and I can only hope that your family is as tender and understanding as my family. Your emotions will be raw and you might inadvertently lob some missiles towards anyone who crosses your path. However, you may have some family members or friends who might take this time, when you are the most emotionally vulnerable, to sort out their _own_ feelings about past hurts and slights that they have been nursing over the years. One of the women in the original cancer support group I attended told me that her *ADULT* son lambasted her on how he felt that he wasn't treated fairly by his parents. He did this even though she was the sole caregiver and her husband was desperately ill due to the cancer and the effects of chemotherapy.

Be forewarned, you might not get the support that you thought you would get from your family or even your children. OK, maybe you didn't buy them a puppy, didn't go to every baseball game because you had to work, didn't bake enough cookies, didn't go to the Girl Scout Jamboree or didn't buy the prom dress they wanted. News flash—everyone needs to kindly climb down from their high horse and get over themselves. Folks, *manure* occurs in life! As adults, people need to learn to turn the page and realize that no one, even a parent, sibling, or friend has an owner's manual in raising children, how to be the perfect brother/sister or friend. We all will make mistakes as parents, siblings, and friends and guess what—*they will make their share of mistakes with their own children, siblings, or friends, too.* You did the best you could with what knowledge you had. Take it from me—try to turn the page and move on with your life.

A few years back, I once watched an interview with Patty Davis, the daughter of President Ronald Reagan, on the Today Show. The interview was regarding her book, *The Way I See It: An Autobiography*. During this interview, she made a statement that has always stuck with me. She said that as long as children blame their parents for what has or has not gone on in their lives; they will FOREVER remain children and not adults. This might not be a direct quote, but it is the gist of what she said. Life is way too short to hold on to all of your negative relationship history. When you die, you are dead for a very long time. Maximize all the good you can grab onto NOW. Only you can decide to hold on to this pain or give it a decent burial.

You don't need any additional stressors in your life at this time when you are not at full strength to handle them. *Again*, *People, if an inner voice says, "Maybe I shouldn't say this, but"*—*THEN DON'T SAY IT!* It is not only unfair, but a cowardly self-serving act to unload your stuff on someone when they are not at their full strength. ***Put your big kid's panties on, build a frigging bridge and cross over it!*** I also saw this happen years ago to my father as he lay dying. The wounds that were created ran deep and it took years to build a bridge long enough and wide enough to cross over again and mend the severed relationships. This advice is warranted to both the grieving person and the family member.

If family members have unresolved issues, they need to find a proper forum to air them. Lobbing grenades and then quickly retreating is not healthy. Group counseling is an excellent option as is agreeing on communication rules that will be put into place so that there is no hitting below the belt or undue drama. Even consider writing a letter. The only problem with letters is that it is a one-way dialogue and so much can be read into a letter. Face to face is best.

Can you tell that I feel strongly about this subject? I do. *REMEMBER: Don't let their stuff become YOUR stuff. End of sermon.*

3) **Changes in Your Routines**

There are many spouses who have to adjust to the everyday aspects of their life. There are husbands who never cooked, who now have to really introduce themselves to the kitchen or the local diner. There are wives who never handled the household finances and find themselves struggling to swim in a sea of unknown financial matters. When you are able to retool your environment, you will be able to resolve your loss. If not, you will remain trapped in your grief process.

One week, I had my two older grandsons with me for three days. I was happy that they were there and told them that I normally don't cook because it is just me and I wasn't going to mess up the kitchen for just one person. Isaac, the family comedian, looked up at me and, at the age of six, started singing "Lonely, so very lonely. You don't have anyone. Poor Miiiimmmmi." We all burst out laughing. Just leave it to Mr. Smart Alec-Isaac to break the tension.

Our family was composed of big-time football fans and we had an intricate football pool which was a source of a lot of fun and bragging. We stopped it the year that Rick became sick. However, one day when I was straightening up around his bed, I found a rough draft of the NFL/AFL scores that he was still attempting to follow. During the year of Rick's death, we stopped our family football pool all together.

After Rick died, I was unable to watch any football, including the 2005 Super Bowl. I just stayed in my son's kitchen and cooked battered-dipped zucchini. My son loved to call Rick during football season and razz him about his beloved Raiders. I told Rick's son, RJ, that if his Dad hadn't already died this year, the way that the 2005 Raiders had played would have surely killed him anyway. Rick and I were avid Sacramento Kings and National Basketball Association fans. I never watched a game the year after his death. It was just too painful for me. I will start to watch the games again, with time but not now.

3) **To Date or Not to Date Might Be the Question**

Our loved ones do not want us to jump into the grave with them. During this stage, our emotional energy has to be redirected towards continuing a productive life. I do not mean that you are to immediately start looking for another spouse. Some people do remarry right away and then regret their knee-jerk reaction. People would surprisingly ask me if I had started dating yet. I thought, "Hey, if I started dating, doesn't that involve holding hands, kissing and other things?" Ewwww! Be in tune with your own emotions. Dating right away will only mask your pain and perhaps lull you into thinking you are healthy enough to move on with this aspect of your life. If you do make this sudden move, you are only setting yourself and your new spouse up for possible disappointment. You have to find ways of redefining your emotional, social, and practical needs by finding new or different relationships and activities. However, if you opt to remarry and move on with your life, you are not dishonoring the love and the life that you shared with your previous spouse.

1st Year Anniversary

Roy, my son-in-law, was very sensitive to me during this time. He suggested that I start a series of "firsts" on key anniversaries that Rick and I shared. On these dates, I need to do something different and then have a new reference for that particular day. I am trying to be aware of these dates and plan something different for them.

During Thanksgiving, I did not change my activities or environment. I stayed at home and cooked the desserts that I typically did ... only Rick wasn't there to peel the apples or taste the dressing. I then went up to my son's and daughter-in-law's home for the holiday and it was a painfully sad holiday for me.

At Christmas, however, I tried to get ahead of this pain. My grandchildren helped me create a Christmas wreath that I took and placed on Rick's headstone during the holidays. Creating the wreath was fun, but I dreaded going to his burial site and placing the wreath on his grave. It is funny how your emotions will protect you. I was concerned that I would have a meltdown at the burial site. Oddly enough, I burst into tears two days earlier just lying in bed deciding what I needed to do that day. This flood of emotions came out of nowhere, but I got it out prior to actually placing the wreath on his grave. As a result, I was not an accident waiting to happen as I traveled down I-5 to Gustine on my way to Los Angeles for the holidays.

While 18 days was a very long time to be away from home, I went on to visit my daughter, her family, and my friend, Mona, in Los Angeles, CA during the Christmas holidays. There were a variety of activities to keep me busy in the Los Angeles area and my pain was not as intense as it was during Thanksgiving. I was pleasantly distracted from my grieving process.

One tradition was definitely missing on this trip. In previous years, Rick, Wendy, Roy and I would play some really competitive Trivial Pursuit as part of our post Christmas visit. It was always the guys against the gals. I used to call Rick "Britannica Senior" and Roy "Britannica Junior" because they both were so dat gum smart. However, they knew never to count Wendy and me out, especially on sports questions. Rick was the resident expert on anything war. However, Wendy and I got a question on who was one of the famous Hitler henchmen whose name started with the letter "G". Wendy immediately shouted out "Gerbil". There was stunned silence. I then looked at her, lowered my voice and said, "Wendy, the name is Joseph Goebbels and not "Gerbil" which is the name of a little rodent." We all fell out laughing while poor Wendy looked like a deer in the headlights! I personally cannot remember laughing so hard in my life. After this, Rick and I could make each other laugh by simply saying the word "gerbil."

On Valentine's Day, I tried to get ahead of the mounting depression. I organized what turned out to be a three-hour luncheon with four other women who had lost their husbands. The ladies had been widows from 15 years to six months. We laughed and cried and shared what we did to deal with our lives after the death of our husbands. One of the ladies had just lost her husband and was really struggling. She was able to see that all of us have struggled as we try to redefine our lives without our spouses. Our milestones were all the same; they just occurred at different times.

During the week of the first year after Rick's death, I went down to Gustine to visit his grave. I had just returned from a fantastic two-week trip to China and had taken off my engagement and wedding rings prior to the trip. When I returned, I opted to move my engagement ring to my right hand. I thought it was appropriate to go to the cemetery and tell Rick. Somehow, in looking back, I think he probably already knew. As I drove into the cemetery, a sad song came on the radio stating that you will never find a love like this again. Tears were welling up in my eyes as I exited the car. I went up to his grave and told him how sorry I was that he had died and that I missed him something awful. It was pretty weird still to see his headstone and know that he was under it in a box—it was all so sad. To commemorate this event:

- I brought down some star gazer lilies that he loved and placed them on his grave.
- I then wanted to prop them up and looked for some rocks to do so.
- I then got some bottled water out of my car to create some mud to hold the rocks that held the flowers.
- Then the tombstone was now muddy, so I had to get some Kleenex out of the car to wash it off.
- Then it smeared, so I needed more water to wash it off.

I know that Rick was shaking his head and thinking, "My wife has lost what is left of her mind." He would often say to me, "Bea, just stop fussing!" Some things don't change, even in death.

It was at this time that I decided that I will now only celebrate his birthday and not the anniversaries of his death.

Counseling

With a degree in psychology and an appreciation for its benefits, I knew that I needed to get some counseling, which I ultimately did. Initially, I went to a group session with a friend who was going through a nasty divorce. The organizers divided us into groups according to our individual situation, i.e., widows/widowers, newly divorced, or separated, etc. This group started out with three people telling the entire group the extremely sad stories and then the organizers would play really depressing my-baby-done-left-me-and-I-want-to die music. Next, they would have a good group cry. *(Oh just shoot me... NOW!)* Afterwards, we would get into our individual groups and the participants talked about how they wanted to kill themselves or after 12 years couldn't part with their loved one's clothing and... on ... and... on. It was like watching one train wreck after another. This type of group may work for some people, but I found myself more depressed AFTER I attended the sessions, so opted out of the remaining ones. I then did some individual counseling and this worked for me. The therapist told me that I was on the right track, but to feel free to check in with her during the holidays because they tend to be a trigger point for a flood of emotions.

GriefShare is another excellent option to handle the grieving process. It is a nationally based program that is composed of a structured 13-week program taking you through the various stages of grief. The program consists of a support group, workbook and video tapes. I co-facilitated this program in the fall of 2007 at my church. It is biblically based, but the concepts are universal and would also help someone who is not a Christian. For more information, you can log onto their website, www.griefshare.org. This program is offered nation-wide and the website can direct you to a GriefShare program nearest you.

The key is to find a therapist or support group that works for you. You may touch bases with several before you find the correct one for you. A friend or associate who has experienced a similar loss is also a valuable find. Make sure these people are not the types who pull you down into their own personal dark deep pit. This is the last thing that you need at this time.

In the fall, I had a need to reconnect with Rick's hospice team. I invited them to tea and we sat around during the lunch hour, reflected on Rick, and shed a tear or two. This support was wonderful and greatly appreciated. His nurse said that she had never taken care of a more humble patient than Rick. He was a one-of-a-kind gentleman. Her comments made me even more proud of him.

Kaiser Hospice was great at monitoring my adjustment during the first year of Rick's death. They followed up with me at Christmas and even asked me to be a speaker for the families at their Remembrance Tree Ceremony. This was a lovely event in which they had Christmas trees with large paper stars that had the names of everyone who had been in their program and who had died during the past year. Sadly, there were a lot of stars on the three trees.

The grief that you will experience will come to you in waves and at unexpected times. Once, I wore one of Rick's shirts to a doctor's appointment. I looked down and saw a stain on it that he made when he dropped some food. I couldn't help but lower my head and cry when I saw the stain. Just a few books that handle the subject of grief are:

SUGGESTED READING MATERIAL

Books	Author
How to Survive the Loss of a Love	Peter McWilliams, Harold H. Bloomfield, and Melba Colgrove
The Grief Club: The Secret to Getting through All Kinds of Change	Melody Beattie
Living with Grief	Kenneth Doka
Understanding Your Grief: Ten Essential Touchstones for Finding Hope and Healing Your Heart	Alan D. Wolfelt and Alan D. Wolfelt, Ph.D.
Winter Grief, Summer Grace: Returning to Life after a Loved One Dies	Miller, James E., Willowgreen Series
Don't Take My Grief Away: What To Do When You Lose a Loved One	Doug Manning
I Wasn't Ready to Say Goodbye: Surviving, Coping and Healing After the Death of a Loved One	Brook Noel and Pamela D. Blair
Letting Go: A 12-Week Personal Action Program to Overcome a Broken Heart	Tracy Cabot and Zev Wanderer
Talking to Children about Death: How To Help Your Child Cope with A Loss	Kaiser Permanente Hospice Fred Rogers
What It Feels Like When A Parent Dies	Jill Kermentz
Talking to Children about Death	Division of Scientific and Public Information, National Institute of Mental Health

There are many great books out there for you to read on how to handle your grief. The Internet and your local bookstore can be your guide in this regard.

Some books might be lighthearted, while others more dry and technical. Picking the correct book for you is like someone else picking the perfect piece of jewelry or art for you because individual preferences will come into play. Where you are in your stage of grief will also dictate which book you might need at this time. You might be drawn to a book just by its title or the author. The books listed above are just a sampling of what is available to you to address your grief and the grief of your family. My suggestion is to cruise by your local bookstore or library and browse the aisles for a book that speaks to you. Also, a simple search on the Internet at the Amazon or Barnes and Noble websites will assist you greatly in this regard.

One strange phenomenon that I found in my case was that the only memories that I had of Rick were the really nice ones. Apparently, this is called "canonization." In my mind, he became "St. Rick." This is what I decided to do. I chose to block out the fights, arguments, and misunderstandings and just opted to concentrate on the good. The rest of the stuff really didn't matter now. I would often second-guess myself. Should I have not listened to the nurse and I have stayed in the room with him until he died? Should I have crawled into the bed and held him until he died? Should I have sung his favorite hymn or prayed over him until he actually died? What if he had had an x-ray earlier on? Should I, should I… you can make yourself nuts if continue to participate in this madness.

An odd situation kept coming up when I had conversations with my two younger grandsons. Christopher and Isaac were four and five years of age during Rick's illness and death. Now, both of these little guys worried constantly about me living alone. On multiple occasions, they would express their concern to me. During a visit to Sacramento from Los Angeles,

Christopher expressed concern over me being by myself. Isaac, being one year older felt it was his place to explain the realities of life to him. He told Christopher that Mimi was going to get a boyfriend, but that he would be old and would die too! Isaac said that he would come and live with me and once he did, all of my dreams would come true! No issue with his feelings of self-worth. I then asked him what his brothers and sister would do without him. He then told me, "no problem" and that his older and younger brother coupled with his parents and big sister could also come and live with me. Well, I thought that this might make HIS dreams come true, but it might be the beginning of my nightmare.

I am confident that you will find some books and counseling options that are perfect for you based upon your stage of grief.

Major Purchases

 I heard from so many sources that no *MAJOR* decisions should be made within a year of the death of a spouse. I am living proof of this. Rick had a fairly new truck that he loved so much. This truck was such a symbol of him and his love of fishing. After he died, just seeing Rick's truck and driving the truck was upsetting to my son, the grandchildren, and me. We looked at the truck and instinctively looked for him. I sold the truck to Carmax and then purchased SUV through them… and took it back five days later. I then had them order me a different SUV and only to take THAT back in five days. Eventually, I kept my 99 Volvo which was in pretty good condition. I was antsy and just didn't know what I wanted. I did a similar thing six months later when I purchased a new washer and dryer and after one washing decided that I didn't like them either. The dealer was very understanding and exchanged them.

Both of my children wanted to know if I was going to move because Rick died in the house. I told them that I wasn't afraid of ghosts and that Rick was always my protector and would not do anything to frighten me. Also, if he were a GHOST, he wouldn't be tied to this house because he would be a … GHOST and could go and be anywhere he wanted to be…ghosts tend to do this. Then I started looking at houses to buy and couldn't find the right one. I would like one that was just a single story. Was there anything wrong with the two-story house I was living in? No… I just was restless and wanted to make changes. I wasn't foolish enough to sell my house and move at this time because my decisions were so unstable. It is a bit more complicated to purchase a house and then want to return it and move back into your original house because you don't like the new one you just up and purchased.

Moving and rearranging THINGS won't impact what is going on inside of you. It simply will take a lot of time for you to make your adjustments. This is a journey that only you can take. You must make this journey on your own, find your own way and do so in your own time.

Get Away

One mistake that I did make was not to take a trip right after Rick's death. My friend, Diana, had called me during Rick's illness and asked me where I wanted to go after his passing. I told her somewhere he and I hadn't gone to... maybe Greece. She said not to worry she would make all the arrangements and four months later we were off to Greece and Turkey. In

retrospect, I should have taken a smaller trip much earlier on to relax. I did go back to my hometown to visit family and friends. I went to attend a funeral of dear older friend and to see her son, Roy D., a friend and Charlene, his wife, whom I hadn't seen in thirty years. While it was great to see them again, this was only one week after I had buried Rick...bad move. It was not what I needed. This was no vacation.

My suggestion is to find a bed and breakfast or visit somewhere fun and relaxing that will provide you with an environment where you won't think about all the madness you have gone through and will have to go through. Go with a friend or go by yourself...but go.

Handling Personal Effects

As stated before, there might be some items that your loved one wants to give away prior to their death or when they die. What do you do with their clothing and other items? This too is a personal decision. I felt that I needed to do something with his things and I was as nervous as a cat on a hot tin roof. So I started bagging, tagging, and giving things away to key family members and friends like a mad woman.

If you opt to donate items to your church or a non-profit organization, you should be able to write these donations off on your taxes under charitable contributions. (Check with your tax professional for details on this subject.) I made a detailed list with a good guesstimate of their reduced value if sold at a second-hand store for tax purposes. It was, however, bittersweet to see family members and friends wearing his things. I know that he would have wanted them to have them and they were pleased to have them, but I did have mixed feelings. When I visit my daughter and son-in-law, I stay in their guest room where Roy keeps a lot of his business clothes. I gave Roy many of Rick's suits and sport coats because they were similar in size. I must confess that on several occasions, I opened the closet door and would gently touch the sleeve of a jacket or suit trying to find just a tiny piece of Rick... to no avail.

During this time, I had been talking to another friend who lost her husband a few months after I did and she was unable to part with her husband's things. This is her decision, and she will handle this aspect of closure in her own time. It is her walk—and I hope that she will be able to move on when she deems it an appropriate time. Everyone has to travel their own path in this regard and not be pushed or goaded into making the transition sooner.

Also, I donated some medical, non-prescription items that we had purchased to a family group home. They welcomed the donation of a walker, cane, etc. I felt good that someone could use these items. Rick was a very generous person and I know that he would have liked this gesture.

Be Honest With Yourself

Fool everyone about your emotional state, if you want to, but don't fool yourself. Continue to stay tuned in to your feelings. For the first time, you will be feeling and facing the reality of death of your loved one. You are quite normal. *Your grief is your grief* and don't allow anyone to tell you to suck it up and get over it.

At Christmas, Wendy and Roy had given me a beautiful mahogany flag holder for the flag I was presented during Rick's burial. It was both beautiful and LARGE. I knew that if I was going to heal and reposition myself emotionally, I could not put this monument to his death up in my house and not continue to be depressed. Was I supposed to sacrifice small animals in front of it or put up fresh fruit and flowers on a daily basis? Regardless of the kind gesture, I knew that I just couldn't have this in the house.

Rick will always be in my heart and in my thoughts, but the flag only reminded me of his death and not the life we had together. I decided to give the flag to his son, RJ, who had been in the military and returned the flag holder for an in-store credit.

When I told RJ that we would be receiving his father's flag, he was blown away and absolutely thrilled. The flag holder has now morphed into a breakfast tray. Wendy, you and Roy are probably learning about this for the first time as you read this chapter but, I know that you will understand.

The world might be telling you that it is time for you to move on with your life, but *it is your life and your loss*. I am sure that your loved one did not and does not want or expect you to jump into the grave behind him/her. They also would not want you to wither away with insurmountable grief.

Moving on with your life is in no way dishonoring your loved one or loving them less, but moving on is a path that you must begin to walk. In time you will be able to do this.

"When your dreams turn to dust, it is time to vacuum".

—*Author Unknown*

Grief, Closure and Moving On
Checklist

Done (X)	Item	Required Action	Status	Comments

Conclusion:

If you have read this book, you are either dealing with the serious illness or impending death of a loved one. In that regard, I empathize with you and you have my deepest, most heartfelt concern.

However, I hope that many of you read this book in an effort to get your affairs in order *prior* to an actual death. If so, you will be way ahead of the curve. *"Farewell, My Friend"* is in fact a manual and a workbook. It should not be something that is read and then set aside. I hope that it will become a book that has lots of entries, catsup marks, donut icing and coffee stains on many of the pages as you pour through the book when you are completing these actions. It should become an active document that you will internalize inside and out as you prepare for the inevitable. Following many of the suggestions and completing the actions will allow you to then get on with the business of living.

I trust that *"Farewell, My Friend"* will help you with your preparation with the death-and-dying process, perhaps ease some of the pain and add clarification. I cannot deny the fact that saying farewell to your loved one will leave scar tissue on your heart. However, while *Dying First Wasn't Part of Their Plan or Your Plan*, you can, with the help of this book, be able to navigate more effectively through the un-chartered waters of illness, dying, death and grief. I have all the confidence in the world that you will be able to do so.

Please feel free to contact me at my blog or website, **bedaparle@farewellmyfriend.net** with any comments or suggestions regarding any subjects this book has covered. I look forward to and welcome your responses.

Thank you.

With Warmest Regards,

Bea

Bibliography and Reference

Book	Author
Final Gifts	Maggie Callanan and Patricia Kelley
Healing Elements of Design a Healing Environment	Nightwood Publication.
Bible	King James Version and New International Version
When Dinosaurs Die	Laurie Krasny Brown and Marc Brown
Journaling the Journey: The Power of Putting it in Writing!	Collette Graves
Life after Death,	Elisabeth Kübler-Ross
How to Survive the Loss of a Love	Peter McWilliams, Harold H. Bloomfield, and Melba Colgrove
The Grief Club: The Secret to Getting through All Kinds of Change	Melody Beattie
Living with Grief	Kenneth Doka
Understanding Your Grief: Ten Essential Touchstones for Finding Hope and Healing Your Heart	Alan D. Wolfelt and Alan D. Wolfelt, Ph.D.
Winter Grief, Summer Grace: Returning to Life after a Loved Ones Dies	Miller, James E., Willowgreen Series
Don't Take My Grief Away: What To Do When You Lose a Loved One	Doug Manning
I Wasn't Ready to Say Goodbye: Surviving, Coping and Healing after the Death of a Loved One	Brook Noel and Pamela D. Blair
Letting Go: A 12-Week Personal Action Program to Overcome a Broken Heart	Tracy Cabot and Zev Wanderer
Talking to Children about Death: How to Help Your Child Cope with A Loss	Kaiser Permanente Hospice Fred Rogers
What It Feels Like When a Parent Dies	Jill Kermentz
Talking to Children about Death	Division of Scientific and Public Information, National Institute of Mental Health
As I See It: An Autobiography	Patty Davis
Military Benefits	http://www.funerals.or/faq/vet.htm.
Social Security Administration	www.socialsecurity.gov
Funeral Costs and Information	http//www.funeralwithlove.com/funeral.htm
Funeral Costs and Information	http://endoflifecare.tripod.com/Caregiving
Funeral Insurance	http://www.cbs.state.or.us/ins/publications/consumer/3932.pdf
Funeral Insurance	http://www.moneymadeclear.fsa.gov.uk/pdfs/funeral_plans.pdf
American Cancer Society	www.cancer.org
American Diabetes Society	www.Diabetes.org
Real Simple	http://www.realsimple.com
Caregivers	Parade Magazine and New England Journal of Medicine.
GriefShare	www.griefshare.org
Academic Paper on Death, 2007	David N Smoke
Medical Advice	www.webmd.com